by Paul Ekman
Professor Emeritus University of California, San Francisco
Founder, Paul Ekman Group LLC

MOVING *Toward* GLOBAL COMPASSION

PAUL EKMAN GROUP
www.paulekman.com

Paul Ekman, Ph.D.

PO Box 26089
San Francisco, CA 94126-0689
Or email info@paulekman.com

ISBN: 978-0-9915636-0-9

FIRST EDITION
10 9 8 7 6 5 4 3 2 1

To the Dalai Lama,
for inspiring me to write this book.

TABLE OF CONTENTS

MOVING *Toward* GLOBAL COMPASSION

CHAPTER 1

Is Global Compassion Achievable?

It would be a different world, a desirable world, if all of us felt *global compassion*: concerned about the suffering of *all* people, not just those in our family, not just those with whom we are familiar, not just those who share the same skin color, language, or religion. Some people do have global compassion, but most don't. The big question is *why not*? Why is global compassion the virtue of the few, not of the many? Is it possible, or even sensible, to try to cultivate global compassion in everyone, or is that a fool's dream?

My friend the distinguished Buddhist scholar Matthieu Ricard used the example of an Olympic javelin thrower to explain his view. We cannot all become Olympic javelin throwers, he said, but we can all improve our ability a bit. Is he right? Or might Matthieu have underestimated human potential? We shall see.

Concern for the suffering of all human beings is asking a lot. But it is central in all the Abrahamic religions.

It is fundamental to what these religions consider to be human. The choice is not between global compassion and no compassion for anyone, between concern for others and concern just for oneself. It is more complicated; there are more choices.

Global compassion need not entirely change our lives, although it does for some people. It does for those who work within Doctors Without Borders or others who choose to live in an area where people face adverse conditions, where many, sometimes all, need help. Even some people who live in an urban metropolitan area in their own country show global compassion when working in homeless shelters or emergency rooms, where those suffering may not resemble them. Some of those working in scientific laboratories to find cures for devastating diseases are motivated primarily by wanting to relieve or prevent the suffering of strangers, not to win a Nobel Prize. They, too, have global compassion, although it is what I call *distal* compassion, or compassion to avoid suffering in the future, and not *proximal* compassion, which is compassion to alleviate suffering felt right now. For all these people, global compassion is the central organizing principle in their life.

Global compassion can and does occur in people for whom it is *not* the central organizing principle in their life but an occasional feature. Global compassion is felt and acted upon, just not all the time, just not determining the major decisions about how and where they lead their lives. Examples are making a donation to help total strangers or taking off a day or part of day to support an organization (such as the Red Cross) that is helping people after a catastrophe. There are many opportunities to contribute something to reduce the suffering of strangers without making that the sole or central organizing principle of one's life.

And yet the harsh reality is that most people do not show even this lesser level of global compassion. Is it too much to expect—will global compassion, even when acted upon only occasionally, be the province of the few? Or could it become the standard, felt and acted upon, at least sometimes, in all or nearly all people? That is ~~the~~ a big question.

Why does it matter? Why does it matter so much to me? There are at least three answers: two completely personal, the last applicable to everyone. My mother committed suicide when I was a teenager. She asked for my help, but I didn't know how to alleviate her suffering. After her death, I was determined to get the education necessary to be able to help others suffering from depression. In time, the scope of my research and my concern extended to trying to improve everyone's emotional life, not just the mentally ill. I found and heralded what is universal about emotional experience, what all people, worldwide, share. Although I didn't think about it in these terms, I was motivated by what I am now calling "global compassion," sparked initially by being unable to help my parent who was suffering severe distress.

The second reason global compassion matters so much to me is more complex. Some parts of it still defy my understanding, although it shapes how I think. It is the result of what happened when I spent five days with the Dalai Lama in the year 2000. Before that meeting I had some disdain for those who paid attention to Buddhism. Many were the same seekers who had earlier become involved with Synanon, Delancey Street, EST, Encounter groups, and Transcendental Meditation, which, one after another, swept through the San Francisco Bay Area during the 1960s and '70s. I watched from the sidelines with some amusement and a little bit of contempt, but I could no longer do that when my daughter got interested in the plight of the Tibetan people.

My wife and I thought we were paying for Eve (then fifteen) to spend five weeks trekking in Nepal, not knowing that it would end with each trekker living for a few weeks in a refugee camp there with a Tibetan family. On Eve's return she organized a high school Free Tibet Club, and because it was so successful, she was invited, with a few other high school organizers, to meet the Dalai Lama.[a]

I knew the Dalai Lama was interested in science and would occasionally invite a small group of scientists to his palace in Northern India for intense discussions. When I learned that invitees were allowed to bring along one silent observer, I thought it would be a treat for my daughter to be in his presence for such an extended period, even if she was only able to listen in. The topic was destructive emotions (none are, I was to

[a] I do not refer to him as His Holiness as others do because I do not consider anyone to be holy, although certainly the Dalai Lama is a very unusual and admirable man.

tell the Dalai Lama; it depends on how you enact the emotion). I submitted my name, was invited, and my daughter Eve and I went in 2000. I introduced Eve as my spiritual leader to the Dalai Lama, explaining that she was why I had come.

Two things soon happened that I still cannot explain. Within a few days I felt a very strong connection develop, as if I had known him all my life and that what mattered to him had to matter to me. I still remember vividly the Dalai Lama saying to the five scientists at a pause in the discussion, "Is this just going to be talk, good karma, or is something going to happen?" He looked directly at me when he said this, and because I had most of my life been almost proud of my pessimism, I was surprised to hear myself say, "I don't know why, but I am no longer a pessimist. As a newly minted optimist, I will try to make something happen." And I did.

I spent the next few years, with the help of many others, organizing *Cultivating Emotional Balance*, a course combining Western and Buddhist understandings of emotion and practices/exercises to improve emotional life. The course lasts forty hours, spread over a number of weeks. Our research was to show it benefited people living a stressful life (as so many of us do).

I had been planning on retiring before that first meeting with the Dalai Lama, but I was not to do so for three more years while Cultivating Emotional Balance grew into existence. Eve now teaches that course, with her own additions to it, in many parts of the world. She and Alan Wallace (the Buddhist teacher responsible for the contemplative part of the training) have taught more than one hundred and fifty people how to teach Cultivating Emotional Balance to others.

Something else occurred during that first meeting with the Dalai Lama that changed my life and defies my ability to explain it. The Dalai Lama would not get up during breaks, allowing this to be a time when observers could ask him questions. On the third day, during such a break, Eve and I sat down on either side of the Dalai Lama while the three of us held hands, and she talked with him for ten minutes. Here is what remains inexplicable: After that meeting, my emotional life was reorganized. My long-standing hatred for my father faded, and my daily efforts to manage too-frequent anger outbursts suddenly were no longer necessary; I felt no anger toward anyone for seven months. In the book the Dalai Lama and I were to later publish in 2008, I offer my attempts to explain how and why this happened. It was the one issue he would not discuss with me. "It is a mystery," was all the Dalai Lama would say.

Over the next five years, I spent more than fifty hours in one-on-one conversations with the Dalai Lama. His passion for compassion became mine as I started to regard him as the brother I never had. At some point he told me he believes we were indeed brothers in a previous life. I remain a non-Buddhist, rejecting reincarnation, among other Buddhist tenets, but there is one Buddhist idea that I have absorbed into my own thinking that is relevant here, for it provides a basis for why we must seek global compassion: *interdependence*. It is the third reason why I believe widespread, worldwide global compassion is very, very important to achieve, if it is possible. And that is a big if.

I always thought that our emotions drive how we relate to others, to those we care about, how we treat them, love them, are afraid of them, and so forth. We are a social species; it is notable when someone lives in isolation. We need others; we are interdependent. How we live our lives influences others, and how others lead their lives influences us. If we believe this is true, it is just one more step toward understanding why we need global compassion.

In the twenty-first century, more than in previous centuries, interdependence is being forced down our throats, like it or not. What we do in some countries affects the lives of others, and what they do affects us. Think of the fires in the Amazon and the hazards created by the smoke that moved to other parts of the world. Consider how the very high consumption of energy and food in Western industrialized countries decreases what is available to others elsewhere. Today, when many are predicting shortages in water, food, and energy, we would have a better chance of making the adjustments that are going to be necessary in order to decrease worldwide suffering if we all felt concerned about everyone's welfare. Those who argue that climate change is going to produce terrible damage to the planet, some of it perhaps irreversible, also would have a more receptive audience if global compassion was the norm, not the exception. It is why I hope that global compassion can become a reality, not a dream.

We must work together to avoid a possible (probable?) disaster for all of us. The more well-off countries must care about the welfare and the suffering of the less well-off countries if we are to jointly decrease our contribution to greenhouse gases. Is that possible? Only if we develop more widespread global compassion. Is it possible? Again, that is the big question.

A distinction I mentioned much earlier in this chapter can help refine the question. When most of us think about global compassion, we have in mind relieving the suffering of someone whom we encounter in the street. If it is global, perhaps it would be an immigrant who has fallen in the street, or someone we read about in the newspaper who is in pain, or a person whose suffering we witness on television. All of these are what I call *proximal* compassion, compassion to relieve suffering in the here and now. But the type of global compassion that is required to lower greenhouse gases isn't proximal, it is *distal*: We act now to avoid suffering in the future. This is what I did when I tried to convince my children to always wear a helmet when they rode their bicycles; I was trying to avoid suffering in the future.

We need distal global compassion to avoid disasters due to greenhouse gases. Distal compassion has two components: recognizing the problem that lies ahead (the distal problem), which depends on accurate social forecasting, and once we recognize the problem, which could be avoided with immediate action, being willing to engage in those actions, even if they require some sacrifices now.

Even in these terms, is it possible that all or nearly all people would ever feel such distal global compassion? Or, again, is that a fool's dream? In kinder words, is it the hope of the optimist, the naïve, the idealist, the radical?

We can't look to science yet for a definitive answer, but there are hints. These hints, however, go both ways: global compassion is the province of the few, or it could be felt by everyone. It may take decades for all the scientific studies and the attempts to cultivate global compassion worldwide to be conclusive one way or the other. Meanwhile, where do you want to put your marbles? I bet you already know which way you are leaning. We don't expect everyone to become Albert Einstein, any more than we expect anyone to become as celebrated as Jay-Z (Bach for the older set) or to play basketball as well as LeBron James (or baseball as well as Joe DiMaggio). If feeling global compassion is also a gift, certain types of evidence should become available if research I outline in the following chapters is pursued. Some might argue that the rarity of global compassion is proof enough that it is a gift, not something everyone would ever feel. But there is evidence that babies have a sense of fairness. And toddlers have been found to try to comfort a stranger showing distress. Could global compassion be there in everyone at the start of life, and if so, why does it fade in most of us?

Before we begin, let me acknowledge where I have put my marbles, what I am hoping the evidence will support: the capability to turn on global compassion, or at least some inclinations in that direction, in everyone.

But those inclinations may not be in everyone, or even in most or many people! I may be wrong, a wishful thinker. We don't know yet.

For those who are neither academics nor scientists, I recommend you read pages 17–25 and then read chapters 4, 5, and 7.

If you want to find out my theory about why some people already have global compassion, with some hints about how to turn it on in others, see pages 47–53.

If you want to find out about the Dalai Lama's reactions to these ideas and how our discussion of them led to a proposal for how the mass media could stimulate global compassion, turn to page 73.

If you want to learn my take on the nature of empathy, turn to page 23.

If you want to learn about five types of compassion distinguished in terms of who the person is that is being helped, turn to page 35.

If you want to find out more about the differences between proximal and distal compassion, turn to page 13.

And, if you want to learn about all of this and more—and read about it in the order I think makes most sense—turn to the next page.

CHAPTER 2

Different Types of Suffering, Different Types of Compassion[i]

In the last few years, there has been a renewed interest in compassion.[50,51,69] Yet focus on how another person's suffering affects our own cognitive and emotional states and behavior is not new. There is a long history of research on related and not often clearly differentiated concepts such as empathy,[3,23,28,29,63] emotional contagion,[58] sympathy,[24] and altruism.[49,55,76,84,86,97,98]

As I explained in the first, introductory chapter, the impetus for what I have written is my conviction that human society must move toward what I am calling *global compassion*: a concern to alleviate the suffering of anyone, regardless of their nationality, language, culture, or religion. It is my hope that by first distinguishing among different interpretations of what the words *suffering* and *compassion* can mean and then developing a typology of compassion, questions will be revealed for research and theory about the nature of compassion, which could start us on new paths in the pursuit of developing more widespread global compassion.

I bring three quite different intellectual traditions to bear: my own more than fifty years of research and writing on the nature of emotion, elaborated and continually enriched by my close observation of the emotions shown in the facial expressions I encounter daily; study of Darwin's writings on emotion and compassion;[18,19,21,42] and the perspective[b] gained from more than fifty hours of one-on-one conversations with the Dalai Lama, both a previously published dialog[17] and new discussions with him about compassion. The combination of these three traditions suggests distinctions and directions, some new, some further elaborations of ideas previously described by others, that may be of help in efforts to cultivate global compassion. In the last pages, I discuss with the Dalai Lama these ideas, and I suggest, and he endorses, a campaign for compassion focused on the entertainment media provided to children.

DEFINING SUFFERING

Compassion is generally understood to be a response to the suffering of another person. But the kind of suffering compassion is aimed at is not a simple matter.

[b] I am not a Buddhist, nor can I claim to be knowledgeable about Buddhist writings on compassion and related states, but I do have the knowledge derived from my discussions with the Dalai Lama and Matthieu Ricard and the benefit of Alan Wallace's review of what I have written.

The Buddhists (pp. 127–128)[100] distinguish three types of suffering. The most obvious suffering is that due to disease or injury, which stimulates pain sensations; included with that is mental anguish not due to an external injury or disease but resulting from interpersonal events, real or imagined. A second type of suffering is more a malaise, a dissatisfaction with life. A third type of suffering refers to the Buddhist view that all human beings are vulnerable to mental suffering, which results from a failure to grasp the interdependence of our existence with the reification of the self's independent and unchanging existence. What I discuss applies directly to the first and to some extent the second type of suffering. What I have written may also be relevant to the third type of suffering, but I am not as certain I understand fully the Buddhist view of this form of suffering, and there are also other practices relevant to this type of suffering.[16,100]

DEFINING COMPASSION

Some definitions of compassion emphasize empathically feeling the emotions experienced by the person who is suffering. I will refer to this as *empathic compassion*. A second focus of compassion is more on the actions that attempt to relieve physical and emotional pain. I will refer to this as *action compassion*. Other definitions describe what can be best characterized as a concern for the person who is suffering, emphasizing the compassionate person's motivation—a desire, urge, or feeling—to alleviate suffering. I will refer to this as *concerned compassion.* The Buddhists describe something somewhat different, a compassion that is more cognitive than emotional, an aspiration or intention.[ii] I will refer to this as *aspirational compassion.*

The value of these distinctions is twofold: it encourages those who train or investigate compassion to specify which type of suffering they are focusing on and which type of compassion they are examining or cultivating. It is my impression that most of the current research and most of the compassion training in the West focuses on the cultivation of empathic compassion and deals with the first type of suffering enumerated earlier: immediately observed physical or mental pain. This is not to deny that some who focus on empathic compassion also add a focus on concerned compassion.

The second benefit of making these distinctions is that it draws attention to questions that could be answered by further research. For example, does action compassion always require first the experience of empathic compassion, or might action compassion be trained directly? Do you need to first feel the target's suffering before you can be motivated to act to relieve the suffering of the target? Another question is whether a primary focus on training concern compassion results in more action compassion? Which type of compassion training results in more compassion for strangers?

Compassion of any kind will not occur unless the compassionate person accurately recognizes that someone is suffering now or is likely to suffer in the future. These two perceptions probably depend on very different psychological processes. The failure to act to prevent future suffering may be the consequence of different events, internal and external, than the failure to act to prevent or alleviate current suffering.

Recent research has shown that those who receive contemplative training are more likely to help a handicapped person experiencing pain.[65,77,93] Very large differences in helping behavior have been found among people observed in different nations, although the cross-national studies, important as they are, dealt more with altruism, or the prevention of future pain, rather than the more traditional focus on relieving someone's pain and suffering.[75]

The *target* of compassion can vary, and in Chapter 4, I will distinguish five types of compassion on that basis: familial, familiars, stranger, global, and all sentient beings. The *immediacy* of the target's suffering also varies, leading me to distinguish between proximal and distal compassion, a distinction that can be applied regardless of the target, so let me reintroduce it now. (I explained it in Chapter 1, but only briefly.)

PREVENTING FUTURE SUFFERING: DISTAL COMPASSION

As a parent, I rarely had the opportunity to prevent immediate physical harm or alleviate physical suffering that was already occurring in my children. Fortunately, neither happened very often. Instead, most of my efforts when they were young were to alleviate, if I could, mental suffering; for example, disappointments in friendship or romantic encounters. A larger part of my efforts was devoted to preventing future suffering; for example, urging that they wear a helmet when riding a bike, warning about the hazards of hard drugs and excessive drinking, and so forth. I did not then construe my actions as compassionate, although what I did met all the characteristics I will describe later for *familial compassion*.

I *had* to do whatever I could to prevent harm from occurring. Once I identified a potential future hazard, I had no choice: I had to plan and act to prevent that harm. It was an involuntary obligation, although sometimes the details of just what was most likely to avert future harm was the subject of some consideration. And I was not always successful in convincing my offspring to take the prescribed actions to prevent future suffering.

Developmental and longitudinal research is needed to determine whether such compassionately motivated acts to prevent future harm are due solely to dispositional or situational factors or the combination of the two. In some circumstances, everyone will realize that suffering is about to occur unless action is taken to prevent an *immediately* impending event; for example, a safe falling from a window that will hit a pedestrian unless the likely victim is pushed out of the way. And yet newspaper reports suggest that not everyone who could act does so, especially if there is any element of risk of harm to the compassionate person.[c]

---

[c] Although the "bystander effect" of being in a group can dilute responsibility, supporting the belief there is no need to act because someone else will do so, being in a group can also increase intervention to help a person at risk.[78]

We do not know whether the observation of impending harm generates compassionate feelings that precede and impel the rescuing intervention in all those who do intervene. If that is generally so for those who do intervene, are those who recognize impending harm but do not act, deficient in *resonance* to the plight of others? Might they have similar compassionate feelings but differ in risk taking or appraisal of the likelihood of risk? Or are such bystanders more generally indifferent to the suffering of others or perhaps to any emotion shown by others? Still another possibility is that those who do not act to prevent impending harm to strangers would do so for familiar or familial persons in danger.

In more complex situations, in which the time between event and harm is not immediate or obvious, only those with the capability for accurate social forecasting may be alarmed. For example, some, but not most, recognized very early in the Nazi regime that eventually the Nazis would harm the Jews, Gypsies, homosexuals, etc. Are those who recognize more remote threats as emotionally aroused and motivated to act on those feelings, as is likely the case of those who act when recognizing the threat of immediate harm? Or might cognition play a stronger role than emotion in such instances? Once the forecast of harm occurs, emotions may then be aroused to motivate the actions that need to be taken to avoid the future harm.[iii]

While recognition of the possibility or likelihood of remote harm may result from unusually good social forecasting, it could also be the consequence of a paranoid outlook, or it could be sensitivity to the plight of all human beings, which is characteristic of a Buddhist orientation toward all sentient life. Do the practices that focus on loving-kindness increase the likelihood of such compassionate acts when the danger is in the future, not the present? When harm is remote, a potential or likelihood rather than a certainty, the failure to act to prevent that harm may result from individual differences in cognitive skills and social outlook rather than a deficit in compassionate emotions, concerns, motivation, or aspirations.

ALLEVIATING CURRENT SUFFERING: PROXIMAL COMPASSION

It is necessary to recognize that someone *is* suffering if one is to intervene to alleviate that suffering. Speech content, vocal signals, and facial expressions may singly or jointly inform an observer that someone is suffering.

There is reasonably well-accepted literature[38] supporting the existence of clear, easily recognized, universal facial expressions of seven emotions (anger, fear, sadness, disgust, contempt, surprise, and enjoyment); of these, the expressions of sadness[iv] are most relevant to identifying someone who is suffering. Both pain and anguish/sadness can be reliably distinguished from one another and from other universal emotions, such as anger and happiness, from vocalizations,[7] and from facial expressions.[39,40,v]

In this research, the facial and vocal expressions are studied out of context in order to determine their signal value, independent of the specifics of any one situation. In real life this rarely occurs. Instead, the situations in which suffering is displayed are typically richly endowed with information that would in itself lead to the judgment that a person in that predicament would be suffering, even if there were no clues from face, voice, or speech.

While the prerequisite for distal compassion is not enabled in all people when the harm is remote and not immediate, the prerequisite for proximal compassion—recognizing when a person is suffering—is enabled in all people, with the exception of those afflicted with specific neurological or mental disorders.

CHAPTER 3

Compassion Joy (CJ) and the Multiple Meanings of Resonance

COMPASSION JOY (CJ)

I propose that it is rewarding, literally, to engage in a compassionate act, proximal or distal, because such actions generate a feeling of joy (I will refer to this as CJ). It feels good, whether or not anyone else knows what the compassionate person has done. It is not merely that such action supports a favorable view oneself.[d] I am proposing it is an emotional feeling, a type of enjoyment that is experienced, independent of benefits to self-image and likely different in physiology than other types of enjoyment.

[d] Harbaugh[57] usefully distinguished between intrinsic and extrinsic benefits for acting compassionately. However, the intrinsic rewards he considers are enhancements of self-image, not the feeling of joy I am hypothesizing occurs when one acts compassionately.

Although not evidence directly for CJ, research on the hormone oxytocin[vi] in relation to trust and empathy is consistent with what I propose. Also consistent (but not proof of) is my proposal that CJ occurs when one acts compassionately, which is another body of research on the neural networks that guide decisions about altruistic or charitable actions.[vii]

Does CJ depend on whether the suffering was relieved by the compassionate person's actions? I suspect that the enjoyment occurs from the act, not the success of the act, but that is a good question for research.[viii,e]

In addition to this good feeling generated by compassionate actions, there are two other benefits. One, already mentioned, is that it supports a positive view of oneself, also a sense of well-being and purpose. The other is that when people learn about the compassionate action, accidentally or by design (for example, a donation to build a hospital for those in poverty, the terms of which include naming the hospital after the donor), their regard for the compassionate person may be increased, and anticipation or knowledge of that increase may generate still a third type of enjoyment in the compassionate actor.

These three benefits I have outlined—an intrinsically good feeling (CJ), an increase in self-regard, and

[e] The distinction between enjoyments such as hearing music, getting a compliment, mastering a difficult problem, and perhaps CJ, all belong to the class of hedonic pleasures. These transient pleasures can be distinguished from more enduring enjoyment referred to as *eudemonia*.[100]

the approval of others—are, from the Dalai Lama's perspective, contaminants, creating a selfish rather than detached motivation, which is necessary for unbiased compassion. By the end of our discussion, he was less concerned about CJ, the intrinsic good feeling generated from a compassionate act, than by increases in self-regard or approval from others.

In other settings, the Dalai Lama has repeatedly said that his compassionate actions benefit him more than they benefit the persons whose suffering are the focus of his compassion, although he did not say, and I failed to ask him, whether he experiences any enjoyment from his own compassionate acts.

RESONANCE

The recognition that suffering is occurring, while necessary, is not sufficient, for it need not inevitably lead to an empathetic response, let alone compassionate feelings, actions, or aspirations. An effective torturer must have accurate emotion recognition to adjust the level of suffering inflicted. Emotion recognition is similar to what those in empathy research refer to as *empathic accuracy* (see Batson, 2011, empathy concept 1)[3]—that is, knowing the emotion the other person is feeling (whether or not you feel it yourself).[64,73] The concept of emotion recognition is more general, subsuming empathic accuracy; emotion recognition does not imply a necessary concern for the person observed, nor does it necessarily imply that the observer will feel the emotion manifest in the person observed.

A prerequisite for proximal compassion, presumed by many who theorize about compassion, is to have an emotional response (not just recognition) to the emotion observed in another person. Some have used the term *resonance* for this phenomenon, but those who use this term have given it a narrow focus: the arousal of just those emotions that are relevant to sympathy, pity, or compassion for the person who is suffering or about to suffer.

Resonance may be better understood as a more general phenomenon, in which *any* emotion observed in another person arouses *any* emotion in the observer. For example, observing another person's amusement may arouse amused feelings in the observer, even when the observer does not know what amused the person observed. Amusement is contagious, but so also are other emotions.[58] Resonance encompasses not just experiencing the same emotion, but also a different emotion than the emotion felt by the person observed. The sight of someone who is amused might arouse contempt in the observer, for example, if the amusement was known to have been evoked by someone's misfortune.

In line with the distinctions drawn by Preston and de Waal's discussion of empathy[87] in nonhuman animals, two quite different forms of resonance can be distinguished: *identical* and *reactive resonance.* In identical resonance,[ix] the perceiver feels, subjectively and physiologically, the emotion that is being felt by the person observed. If that person is angry, the perceiver feels and shares that anger; if the person observed is afraid, the perceiver feels and shares the fear. In identical resonance, the observer is driven by feeling what the observed person is feeling[24] and is potentially supported by emotional mimicry, the automatic tendency to copy another's facial expressions,[x] and perhaps enabled by mirror neurons. This notion is similar to what has been labeled *emotional empathy* or *emotional reciprocity* by other researchers,[64,99] whereby the individual shares to some extent the feeling state of the target, and it is posited that this shared feeling plays a crucial role in compassionate responding. This type of compassion can be considered, from this vantage point, an instance of identical resonance, in which the feelings observed and resonantly experienced are the manifestations of suffering.

However, compassionate feelings and aspirations might be composed of *concern* for the suffering person, not requiring that the compassionate person feel the sufferer's suffering. Concern is generally considered to be a variant of the emotion fear.[39,40,41,66] I don't know of any research that has tried to identify whether both occur in the same individual, or if some compassionate people experience suffering, while others experience concern.[f]

The occurrence of identical resonance could lead to compassionate feelings and actions regardless of what emotion is shown by the person observed. For example,

[f] Rosenberg et al. (in review)[90] suggest it is suffering that predominates, but the data has not been analyzed in a way that would determine if concern or worry also occurs in the same or different people.

sharing the observed person's anger toward a third party could lead the observer to help the person observed deal with a provocation and thus be considered compassionate. This type of resonance is not what has been focused on in past theory and research that has considered resonance or concepts akin to it. Instead, research has focused on identical resonance, in which the observer feels the pain or suffering of the person observed, taking the perspective of the sufferer without becoming or merging with the sufferer.

Theorists since Darwin[18] have argued that the experience of distress when viewing another's pain or suffering motivates compassionate actions. Darwin wrote, "We are . . . impelled to relieve the sufferings of another, in order that our own painful feelings may be at the same time be relieved" (p. 129).[22] Although it is unlikely that Darwin's views were informed by knowledge of the Buddhist view,[42] it is remarkably similar. Recently the Dalai Lama said, "In the human mind, seeing someone bleeding and dying makes you uncomfortable. That is the seed of compassion" (p. 197).[17]

By calling this the "seed of compassion," the Dalai Lama maintains that no such selfish benefit persists in the development of compassion through loving-kindness meditative practices, the goal of which is unbiased compassion—no benefit to the compassionate person for acting compassionately. Even though the compassionate person feels good as a consequence of wishing to relieve suffering, it is not her motivation for acting.

Both Darwin's and the Dalai Lama's accounts of the *origins* of the motivation for compassion suggest that such actions serve a selfish, self-focused adaptive end—reducing the observer's own suffering, felt in response to witnessing the suffering of the person observed. Still another benefit is the possibility I have suggested that altruistic or compassionate actions generate positive feelings (CJ) in the person engaging in such deeds.

It is not known exactly what type of positive feeling is generated within the person who acts compassionately. Is it the same or different from any of the sixteen[g] possible enjoyable emotions that I have enumerated, all of which I have posited are different one from another. Enjoyment of any kind motivates repetition of the action that generated the feeling. What I am calling *compassion joy (CJ)*, once experienced, may contribute to sustaining a compassionate outlook. In some people, compassionate actions may be solely motivated by the desire to experience CJ, just as some may act compassionately to win the admiration of others.

Another possibility is that compassion joy is the indirect result of being able to maintain a positive self-regard for having engaged in such actions.[6,27] That, too, could motivate compassionate actions. That, too, would contaminate the Dalai Lama's aspiration for

[g] The sixteen different types of enjoyment, some of which may be considered to be emotions, include the five sensory pleasures, as well as amusement, contentment, excitement, relief, wonderment, ecstasy, *fiero* (the enjoyment resulting from a difficult achievement), *nachus* (enjoyment aroused by accomplishments of one's offspring), schadenfreude, elevation or rejoicing (enjoyment from witnessing compassionate or heroic actions by others), and gratitude.[41]

uncontaminated compassion, in which the motivation is not influenced by any benefit to the self.

There is a second quite different type of resonance that may serve to motivate compassionate feelings and/or actions. A person's distress or pain might elicit a different type of emotion in another rather than a shared response (cf. the notion of emotional complementarity).[99] In reactive resonance, the perceiver experiences an emotion in response to, but not the same as, the emotion displayed by the other person.[xi]

Reactive resonance need not motivate compassionate feelings or actions. Enjoying the sign that someone is suffering is reactive resonance that would not be likely to lead to compassion. More than forty years ago,[37] I found that about a third of the people observing a medical training film responded with disgust to the sight of blood and surgical scenes, the same proportion in Japan and the United States. It seems less likely that this resonant response would lead to actions to reduce suffering—as one typically pulls away from the source in disgust—but there is no research to show that is necessarily so. Is a disgust response to the physical manifestations of pain a stable, enduring personal characteristic, or might it be, in at least some people, an initial response, soon followed by a more sympathetic form of resonance?

A clearer instance of reactive resonance that should be conducive to compassionate actions was mentioned earlier, positing that some observers feel *worry* or *concern* (both classified by most standard dictionaries as variations within the fear family of emotions) by the observed person's suffering. Presumably a person could be concerned about someone's suffering and not feel any need to act to relieve it, but that is unlikely. One could know that someone was experiencing pain from an untreatable condition, be concerned about that person's suffering, but know that there is nothing he or she could do to alleviate the suffering. I do not know of evidence that concern about another person's suffering is indeed always bound to and intrinsic to a desire to relieve that suffering (if possible), in all people, but that would seem likely.

I believe reactive resonance involving concern to relieve suffering is very similar if not identical to what Batson has called *empathic concern*, which he says is resonance that is "congruent with the perceived welfare of someone in need" (p. 12).[3] While Batson writes that it may involve any emotion as long as the focus is on the other person's welfare, I expect the emotion would be some variation of worried concern or sadness.

Do those who are not sympathetic to the suffering of others (another term for describing resonance linked to the wish to alleviate suffering) manifest a more general deficit in resonance? Is this the case in what has been described as burnout? That literature suggests resonance to another's suffering and the motivation to relieve that suffering can be extinguished when there is an overload of suffering that is observed and the observer believes there is no way to relieve that suffering. Are people who experience burnout in their work setting indifferent to any emotion shown by any person, or is such a deficit more specific to a particular situation, a particular type of person? Or is it more emotion-specific, for example, responsive to all emotions but not to suffering?

It is worth noting that empathic concern may play a lesser role, not as intensely felt in distal compassion as compared to proximal compassion. In distal compassion, there may also be a less intense experience of what I earlier called compassion joy. However, the benefits to self-image and the regard of others should be as rewarding in distal compassion as they are in proximal compassion. Quite apart from the immediate pleasure felt when acting compassionately (what I have called CJ), there may also be pleasure felt when one observes the beneficiary of one's compassionate actions suffer less. This source of pleasure would be absent in distal as compared to proximal compassion.[xii]

Darwin tried to explain the failure of some people to be motivated to alleviate the suffering of others: "It is evident in the first place, that with mankind the instinctive impulses have different degrees of strength; a savage will risk his own life to save that of a member of the same community, but will be wholly indifferent about a stranger" (p. 134).[22] Preston and de Waal wrote, "The more interrelated the subject and object, the more the subject will attend to the event, the more their similar representations will be activated, and the more likely a response. The more similar the representations of the subject and object, the easier it is to process the state of the object and generate an appropriate response" (p. 5).[87]

Television news searches the world for instances of suffering to display in what is assumed to be in some fashion entertaining. Presumably most people do not enjoy what they see, but are, for reasons not obvious, attracted to and fascinated by observing the suffering of others. Television companies would not show people suffering if such displays did not attract viewers.

Do those television viewers feel compassion toward those they see? The donations that occurred without solicitation to Japan's 2011 tsunami disaster suggest a positive answer. And there are many similar, although less heralded, actions. But not by everyone who is attracted to and watches suffering. What is the emotional experience of these people who seek to view suffering on television but take no action to relieve the suffering of the people they see or others? What is their motivation for watching these scenes of suffering?

Some people may experience resonance when observing *some* or all people who are quite dissimilar. Early childhood experiences with the caregiver have been offered as the explanation for why some people resonate to the suffering of strangers.[34,50,87,h] This should be regarded as a hypothesis, requiring longitudinal research to confirm. I return to this issue when I consider how to cultivate compassion for strangers (see Chapter 5).

[h] Eve Ekman elaborated this view: "Attachment theorist suggest that too much exposure to indifference, neglect, and disorganized caregiver behavior can create reactive, splitting, and disorganized adult relationships."

CHAPTER 4

Distinguishing Compassion in Terms of the Target

IS COMPASSION AN EMOTION?

Those who are not, like me, students of emotion, might wonder why the answer to this question matters. The answer is that we have learned a great deal about the nature of emotions in the last few decades.[xiii] If compassion is another emotion, we would know quite a bit about what features would be inherent in it, given what we know about emotions such as anger, fear, enjoyment, etc.

The type of compassion that most closely resembles what is known about emotions is *familial compassion*, exemplified by the mother's compassionate concern to relieve the suffering of her baby. Using the distinctions I have drawn so far, the type of familial compassion that would be the best candidate to be considered one of the emotions is *proximal* (not distal), focused on compassionate *feelings* (not actions[xiv]). Distal familial compassion involves cognition much more than emotion and is not as likely a candidate to be considered one of the emotions.[i]

Darwin wrote, "... young and timid mother urged by the maternal instinct will, without a moment's hesitation, run the greatest danger for her own infant" (p. 134).[22] The Dalai Lama said, "... in those animals, like turtles, no dealing with mother. I do not think they have the capacity to show affection" (p. 146).[17] "[To cultivate compassion] . . . you deliberately try to develop attitude—as dear as your own mother" (p. 163).[17]

Certainly this type of familial (proximal, feelings) compassion exhibits many of the characteristics that I proposed[39] distinguish emotions from other types of mental life: It appears to be an unbidden involuntary response—immediate in the sense that it occurs as a result of a very fast appraisal—and it is not unique to humans but found in other primates. Two other characteristics of emotions are likely but not yet investigated: distinctive thoughts, memories, and images associated with this mental state, and the existence of a refractory period, in which attention is focused on the matter at hand, filtering out all information not relevant to relieving the suffering offspring.

There are two more characteristics of the emotions that may be present in familial compassion, but the

[i] From the Buddhist view, familial compassion would likely involve intense aspiration to relieve suffering but not an emotion (Wallace, personal communication, 2013).

evidence is not robust. There have been reports of a unique signal, which can be quite brief, and universally recognized, but the evidence is not clear-cut.[xv] The failure to have a distinctive signal should not be regarded as sufficient grounds to say that familial compassion is *not* an emotion, since a few other mental states judged to be emotions by most theorists also do not have a unique signal—shame and guilt, for example.[xvi]

The other characteristic found in emotions but not certain in familial compassion is a unique pattern of physiology. It has yet to be established that the physiology observed in familial compassion is different from that found in the compassionate feelings experienced about the suffering of a friend or the observance of pain, sadness, or anguish in someone with whom one is intimate but is not a family member. A number of recent investigations have identified patterns of neural activity that precede or accompany proximal compassionate feelings, but it is not yet known whether that activity is unique to compassion or found with other related experiences, such as experiencing suffering oneself.[70,79,103] I think it is best for the time being to remain agnostic about whether there is both a distinctive signal and physiology for familial compassion.

The biggest difference between familial compassion and the emotions is the necessity to indicate the target in its naming: familial. Anger, fear, or disgust, for example, can be felt toward anyone or anything. Familial compassion is restricted to one target: a family member. And further, it is restricted to only one event in that family member: suffering. By contrast, anger or fear can be felt toward any target, anyone or anything, and not by a specific mental state of the object. In anger and fear, the focus is on the person feeling that emotion—the angry person's pursuits are blocked in some way, and the angry person feels frustrated or provoked by the other, just as the fearful person feels endangered by the other's actions. In compassion, the focus is on helping the other, not the self.

It is not known whether familial compassion is felt as strongly in response to the suffering of an adult offspring as an adolescent, as strongly toward the suffering of an adolescent as toward the suffering of a child, or toward a child as strongly as toward the infant. Does increasing independence decrease the compassion felt toward a family member? With an infant or toddler, the parent can provide protection and guidance in a near complete fashion. With an adolescent or adult, a parent is no longer so enabled and usually can do no more than provide support, worry, concern, and advice in most contexts.

The boundaries of familiar compassion are not known. Is its strength an inverse function of increasing distance in the genes shared between the observer and person observed?[j] Is familial compassion as intense and immediate for offspring, siblings, parents, cousins, uncles and aunts, or grandparents? Might the strength of familial compassion be determined not by genes

[j] Adoption studies I expect would reveal that shared genes are not necessary for strong familial compassion, but I know of no studies of compassion in adoptive parents. Thanks to Clifford Saron for raising this question.

shared but by the amount of intimate contact shared? We don't know the range of individual differences in the scope and strength of familial compassion or the factors that might determine such differences.

The second characteristic of emotions that may not occur in familial compassion is that compassion is considered to be always constructive, while each emotion can be enacted either constructively or destructively. We shall see that the matter is more complicated.

The criteria we[17] proposed for whether any emotional episode is constructive or destructive is whether it furthers or impedes future collaboration among the participants and whether the collaboration is of benefit to society.[k] Even amusement should not be considered always to be a constructive emotion, if the amusement is in response to another person's humiliation or amusement is blended with or provoked by ridicule.

In my first meeting with the Dalai Lama in 2000, he asked me if compassion could ever be destructive. Without having considered the matter before, I replied that the overprotective parent who could not grant the growing child increasing autonomy would be such an example.[52] Now I would answer differently. Proximal familial compassion that attempts to alleviate the observed suffering of the child is always constructive. The overprotective parent would be engaging in distal

[k] I thank Alan Wallace for pointing out the need to add this second feature. Good collaboration among those planning terrorism would have to be considered constructive without this addendum.

familial compassion, constricting the child's freedom to avert possible future suffering, which I would judge as destructive in consequence but not in motivation. There are many explanations in the parent-child literature of both the harmful effects of overprotection and the motivation behind it.[1]

Regardless of whether we consider familial compassion to be an emotion, there is no question that it is vital when an organism's survival early in life depends, as it does for mammals and some other species as well, on the commitment of a caretaker. Kin selection, the evolutionary mechanism that prompts individuals to help their close relatives or kin so that they will survive to reproduce and pass on related genes to their offspring,[56] may support familial compassion. Helping has been found to be more likely for individuals genetically closer to the helpers.[54]

Familial compassion is not a one-time event; whether it is proximal or distal, it is an enduring feature, even when not evident, and it is ready to be called up when there is suffering, or a threat of suffering, or the anticipation of future suffering of the offspring. Like the emotions, it is universal to the species, permanently in place, and like the emotions, it can be observed in other species. There are exceptions—parents who do not experience familial compassion—and various explanations for why and when this occurs.

[1] From the Tibetan Buddhist viewpoint, overprotection is a manifestation of a lack of wisdom. For an in-depth presentation of the Tibetan Buddhist view, see Patrul Rinpoche.[89]

FAMILIARS COMPASSION

Both distal and proximal compassionate feelings and actions may be aroused by familiar people. Not all familiar people may evoke a compassionate response, with large cultural and individual differences very likely. Presumably, the closer the relationship, the more acknowledged interdependence, the greater the likelihood that familiars compassion will be felt (although I know of no evidence that this is really true).

STRANGER COMPASSION

While some might still argue that familial or familiars compassion is best considered among the emotions, there should be little dispute that *stranger compassion* is not. Unlike familial or familiars compassion, it is *not* universal to our species or to any other species (later in this section, I will explore the possibility that stranger compassion may be universal early in life but not sustained without certain later experience[m]).

Stranger compassion, like familial and familiars compassion, is not unique to humans. Emotions may distort perception, but it is said that stranger compassion does not. Emotions can be momentary, while distal stranger compassion is not.

[m] Even if that is so, and it is far from established, such possible stranger compassion early in life appears to be much more fragile than the emotions that persist throughout life, unless there is exceptional trauma.

Stranger compassion varies in the scope of those toward whom it is felt. It may encompass only those who share some characteristic, such as race, religion, geographic region, etc. Stranger compassion also varies in the centrality or degree to which that concern is the organizing principle behind a person's life choices. It can range from an occasional act of compassion to, at the other extreme, the motivation that guides a person's life work, geographic location, etc. When the compassion is felt toward *all* human beings, and it is a *central* concern in a person's life, I call it *global compassion.*

Stranger compassion has been found, in a remarkable series of experiments, to vary across nations, with people in Rio de Janeiro and Mexico City the most compassionate and New Yorkers the least. Both cultural factors and population density appear to explain why these differences were found.[74,75] These studies examined proximal compassionate actions; it is likely, but not known, that the same findings would pertain to distal compassion.

Recent studies have documented stranger compassion in toddlers who, without prompting, console an unfamiliar distressed person.[91] Such compassion emerges in the second year of life.[xvii] Both genetic and environmental effects have been found, with their relative contribution changing over time.[71]

It would be important to also determine when such early stranger compassion begins to disappear. Do the recent studies that children form in-group/out-group determinations as early as four years old[31] imply that consoling would become less prevalent toward those strange children recognized as out-group members? If a child is exposed early to other children of various demographic characteristics, would the in-group/out-group distinctions still emerge? At what age does stranger compassion become the exception rather than the rule? (The age at which this becomes evident and why this might be so remain to be determined.)

SENTIENT COMPASSION

Darwin wrote, "Sympathy beyond the confines of man, that is, humanity to lower animals, seems to be one of the latest moral acquisitions . . . This virtue, one of the noblest with which man is endowed, seems to arise incidentally from our sympathies becoming more tender and more widely diffused until they extend to all sentient beings" (p. 147).[22] His emphasis on the importance of sentient compassion is similar to the Buddhist view, but not a result of knowledge of those writings.[42] Although many questions about the relationship between sentient and stranger compassion could be raised, they are beyond the scope of this discussion and the expertise of this writer.

HEROIC COMPASSION[xviii]

Rather than being a different type of compassion, as those enumerated so far, heroic compassion is a subset of each of those forms of compassion: global, stranger, familiar, or familial compassionate actions. The distinguishing feature is that the compassionate action might endanger the life of the person who acts. It is thought to be common for risky compassionate action to be shown by a parent toward an offspring who either is in danger of immediate harm or is already being harmed and obviously suffering. Heroic compassion can be either proximal or distal.

Darwin wrote, ". . . many a civilized man, or even boy, who never before risked his life for another, but full of courage and sympathy, has disregarded the instinct of self-preservation and plunged at once into a torrent to save a drowning man, though a stranger" (p. 134).[22] In this example, Darwin notes that heroic compassion is shown by other animals.[26]

Most people do not know if they have heroic compassion, never having been in a situation in which there was a need for a risky rescue. Political scientist Kristen Monroe[83,84] studied individuals who engaged in a single act of heroic compassion, comparing them to those who hid Jews in Nazi occupied countries and with philanthropists whose actions benefited others without putting their own lives at risk. She points out that those who rescued Jews put not only their own life but also the lives of family members and sometimes entire villages at risk.

In the terms I have introduced, Monroe examined stranger compassion, both proximal compassionate acts (those who acted once to rescue or relieve someone who was suffering) and distal compassionate acts (those who hid Jews from the Nazis). She focused on actions not just feelings of compassion.

Monroe applied five criteria for classifying a behavior as heroic compassion: it must involve an act, not just a thought or feeling; the goal is the welfare of the person in danger; the action taken has consequences for that person; there must be some risk for the person taking action; and the action is taken with no expectation of reward or recognition.

She found no differences between the philanthropists and those who showed heroic compassion in age, sex, religion, or education. She found the major difference between those who were heroic and the philanthropists was in what she called their "worldview."[n] Here are examples of what she called their worldview, taken from her interviews: "You help people because you are a man and you see a need; we all belong to one human family . . . all people have value." They also differed in that the heroic said they believed it was not a matter of choice, they had to do it: "They needed help. I had to do it"; "I had no choice." Psychological measures were not obtained in her study.

It appears from Monroe's research and from many newspaper reports of heroic compassion that sometimes the heroic act occurs within fractions of a second of observing danger or suffering. There is not time for conscious registration of compassionate feelings prior to the rescue. The motivation for these heroic actions must be sought elsewhere.

Not much is known about why some people evidence heroic compassion toward strangers, although

[n] Although this is the same term used by Buddhist theorists about compassion, in conversation with Monroe, I verified that she was not familiar with those writings and derived this concept quite independently.

there is little doubt that it is shown by only a minority of people and a minority of other animals. Does it occur in all primates? And just in primates? Detailed observations of orangutans suggest that stranger altruism toward members of their own and other species may be normative, not exceptional.[95] More observations are needed, for this is an extraordinary possibility.

If one member of a family has shown heroic compassion toward strangers, is it likely that it will be manifest in other family members? Is it more common in both of the identical twins than in both fraternal twins? Are there particular cultural backgrounds that generate a higher incidence of such heroic compassion? Are there any commonalities in the early experiences of those who later are heroically compassionate toward strangers? What are the characteristics of newly formed small groups that later produce someone who confronts danger to the group with heroism as compared to groups that confront danger without anyone acting heroically?

All of these same questions can be asked of why some, but not most, people show stranger compassion. As I have described it, stranger compassion is best viewed as two sets of orthogonal continua: one of these continua ranging in *scope* (all strangers, as in what can be called global compassion, or just some strangers, such as fellow Americans) and the other continua ranging in life *centrality* (occasional acts, or life choices).

CHAPTER 5

Why Do Only Some People Show Stranger Compassion?

I don't think a database currently exists on those people who have organized their lives around a career of stranger compassion, such as those who chose to spend their lives providing services to impoverished peoples in quite adverse environments. Nor have interviews been done to check the same demographic information that Monroe investigated in her study of heroic compassion.[83] I expect the findings would be the same: no differences in demographic characteristics and no single factor that explains why these people, and not a matched control group, committed themselves to a life of stranger compassion. Such an investigation is very much needed.

My hunch is that those who devote their lives to compassionate actions will, when asked why they made this choice, provide the same answers that parents would if asked why they acted compassionately toward their toddler. It will resemble what Monroe found for her heroically compassionate rescuers of Jews—they had to do it; it wasn't a choice; it was a necessity.

Whether or not my hunch is correct, the question remains why some people manifest stranger compassion while most people do not, or at least do not organize their lives around a devotion to stranger compassion. Is it mere chance, not explicable in any known terms? Or might it be something in the upbringing of these people? Only longitudinal studies could answer that if we are not to rely on retrospective reports. Longitudinal studies would also reveal how early in life such compassionate concern was first evident.

Certain forms of meditative practices have been found to enhance compassion toward strangers.[13,68,69,90,103] All of these studies focused on proximal compassion; some examined compassionate feelings, but others examined compassionate actions.

Many questions remain about this burgeoning body of research. The data is not reported in a way to determine whether the increased compassion is shown by everyone or just the majority of the group given training. And, if it is not evident in everyone, what might account for who responds and who does not? It is not known how long this meditative practice must be followed, nor whether compassion endures after a period of time with no practice. Nor has there been study of whether contemplative practices generate truly global compassion, toward strangers who differ in appearance, language, and culture.

And perhaps of most importance for evaluating this body of research is the failure to control for *demand characteristics.*[xix] The late Martin Orne is known for raising the possibility that findings on hypnosis might be attributed to the demand characteristics of the contexts in which it was being studied.[104] Orne asked a group of subjects to act the way they thought hypnotized subjects would act. These nonhypnotized subjects produced all the findings attributed to hypnosis. To be certain that the findings obtained to date on the benefits of compassion training cannot be attributed to demand characteristics, subjects need to be told about meditative practices, given no meditation training (just the information on what it is about and what its goals are), and then asked to act on the various outcome measures that have been used in research on meditation, as if they had been given meditative training. I think it is important to also include such a demand characteristics control in the studies that have examined the physiological changes that occur during meditation, for it is possible that subjects so instructed might show changes in brain activity that resemble (how closely needs to be discovered) the changes observed in those who do receive meditative training.

To the best of my knowledge, all of the scientists who have conducted research on meditation are either meditators themselves or strong believers in the benefit of contemplative practice. This opens the possibility of unwitting experimenter bias. To guard against potential bias, when I conducted a series of studies on war and peace in the 1960s–1970s, I explicitly balanced the bias by recruiting on each research team scientists who disagreed with each other about the matter at hand. They had to agree on how the study was performed, including data collection and analysis, and later on the paper that was written. I strongly urge that an attempt be made to "balance the bias" in future research on how to generate compassion.

Even if demand characteristics and unwitting experimenter bias can be ruled out, if the goal is to increase global compassion worldwide in the foreseeable future, contemplative practice may not be a practical route (not that there are other more practical routes to propose). It is costly in time and so not likely to be adopted on a worldwide basis, unless it was to be incorporated into primary or secondary school education. The fact that it is derived in large part from Buddhist practices will make it difficult for public schools to adopt it in some countries, even if it is presented in a secular fashion.

A second line of research should be pursued, although it also is not likely to suggest practical steps that can be readily adopted to generate global compassion throughout the world. Some people have global compassion without any prior contemplative practices. And we don't know why.

Perhaps some genetic factors predispose individuals to have stranger compassion? Certainly recent studies identifying genes predictive of helping behavior suggest this may be so.[15] It may well be a combination of genetic factors activated by specific environmental circumstances.

Now consider a Western, psychological explanation, albeit one also not grounded empirically (although it is subject to test, as I will explain). I have proposed that human beings possess an *emotional alert database*, comprising triggers that, through automatic appraisals, instigate emotional impulses.[41,43] The exact nature of those triggers, whether they are scenes, scripts, or a fixed sequence of evaluations, is not germane to the issue here, but what must be granted is that some of those triggers are universal to the species, representing what Lazarus called the "wisdom of the ages," established as a result of repeated experiences over generations in our ancestral environment. These are the unlearned triggers, such as a sudden loss of gravity triggering fear.

Most triggers, however, are learned, entering the emotional alert database as a result of various emotional experiences over the course of one's life. I believe (based on LeDoux's[xx] research, personal experience, and observation) that it is very difficult to erase a learned trigger, once it has entered the emotional alert database. It can be weakened through various practices,[xxi] but will reappear when stress seems to enliven weakened learned triggers.

One step more in this line of explanation is the proposal that offspring, perhaps just infants, are an unlearned trigger for familial compassion. And that in some people it is not just their own offspring but all people who are regarded in the same way—they are all family; they are all unlearned triggers for compassionate actions in the emotional alert database.

Support for this proposal comes from Monroe's study. Although I do not know of a similar database for familial compassion, I suspect that if asked, parents would use similar words to explain why they engaged in familial compassion, as did her rescuers of total strangers, and would, like them, say that they had no choice, and that they had to do it.

My own experience supports my expectation, although my data is a recollection, not gathered at the moment. Only once in my own life was there a need for heroic compassion—to rescue my daughter as a toddler from an oncoming car. I recall no thought, no consideration before I acted, rescuing her by actions that endangered my life. It was involuntary action. If asked why I did it, I would have said, "I had no choice. I didn't think about whether to act or not; I acted." Like most people, I have not yet been in a situation calling for heroic compassion to rescue a stranger, and so I do not know if I would act as I had for a family member.

I have been considering the possibility that *some* people have, for inexplicable reasons, the suffering of all people, not just family members, in their emotion alert database. Alternatively, it might be that everyone has the suffering of all people, all strangers, in their emotional alert database, but it needs to be awakened. This could occur by an emotionally intense event or trauma, or a national trauma such as 9/11, or an inspirational encounter with someone who has global compassion. The proposal is that everyone has the potential, but it must be activated in most people. It is only in a minority of people that it is activated, but the hypothesis is that the potential is there in everyone, awaiting activation. Within this more generous or optimistic formulation, it is still necessary to explain this difference—why is global compassion active from early life in some, but not most, people without some special event activating it? At the end of this chapter, I will attempt an answer to this question.

Although not central to my line of reasoning, let me point out some similarities between the explanations I have offered for why global compassion is active in some people to an explanation, as I understand it, based on reincarnation.

Although arising from entirely different traditions, both the reincarnation and the psychological explanations share some fundamental propositions about human nature. Both assert that the past influences the present, that how someone acts today is not solely determined by his or her choices, conscious or unconscious, but by the past. Both explanations, more specifically, suggest that past lives, the lives of one's ancestors, influence how one behaves today.

These explanations are the exact opposite of the Lockian view that human beings are tabula rasa, with nurture not nature creating and determining how one leads one's life. Neither the reincarnation nor the genetic explanation of stranger compassion rules out the influence of nurture, it is just not the sole determinant.

While traditional science cannot investigate reincarnation, it can determine, as mentioned earlier, the psychological/genetic explanation by twin studies, checking on the incidence of stranger compassion across generations and longitudinal studies starting early in life. My hunch is that genetics may predispose a person to develop global compassion, but it won't be activated without certain life experiences. While it is beyond my expertise to suggest what those experiences might be, longitudinal research should help to clarify this.°

HOW CAN GLOBAL COMPASSION BE INCREASED?

In industrial societies in the nineteenth and twentieth centuries, it was possible to focus solely on one's own welfare, accumulating material wealth without regard for its impact on others—the rugged individualist, capitalist worldview. The political judgments of many today are that such a worldview is no longer viable, that we do live in a global village, and that the Buddhist concept of interdependence is literally true in terms of how we individually choose to treat our environment. Those who warn about global warming and impending shortages in food, water, and energy argue that the adjustments in lifestyle and use of resources necessary to avoid disaster require a compassionate concern for every human being's welfare—global compassion.

The Abrahamic religions urge global compassion, but it is not certain that such teachings play a role in

° Eve Ekman (personal communication) suggested the need for research to identify obstacles to compassion; for example, the over-arousal of stress. Which led me to wonder whether there is any deficit in compassion among those who have been afflicted with PTSD?

creating stranger compassion. Certainly they do not do so for most people; and those who do exhibit global compassion might be so predisposed, drawn to religious teachings because they support their compassionate inclinations, not because they create those inclinations. It is unlikely that religious training, as it is presently practiced, will increase global compassion.

Even if research were to support the role of genetics in predisposing some people toward global compassion, it is not obvious how that finding could help those who want to increase the frequency of this behavior. It would be helpful to discover whether there are certain life experiences that occur in most people who exhibit global compassion, pointing toward what is required to activate a genetic predisposition, if indeed there is such a predisposition in all people.

There are now many different approaches to cultivating compassion, many of which are being evaluated through research. Admittedly, I only know about some of this work, for there is a lot of it worldwide, but I believe the focus is primarily on proximal compassionate feelings, much less on actions, and very little on distal compassion. Recent research[70] suggests that loving-kindness contemplative practice generates different neural circuits than contemplative practices focused on empathy, but did not examine differences between the two in the likelihood of compassionate actions. This research needs a control for demand characteristics, which I described earlier on page 77, and also for unwitting experiment bias.

It is much too early to know which focus (distal or proximal, feelings or actions) and which approach to increasing whatever is focused on will be most successful. The most successful approach for cultivating global compassion may vary with the focus, the circumstances, and the individuals addressed. I think it likely that efforts focused on actions to prevent suffering (distal actions) will be most successful, across various people, if it occurs in late childhood and adolescence. Distal not proximal compassion is likely to be more educable by traditional means, since distal compassion is probably determined more by cognition, by values, judgments, forecasting, and so forth, than is proximal compassion.

Earlier I proposed that there are three quite different positive consequences that an individual might experience after engaging in a compassionate action (perhaps just from the compassionate feelings, even if not acted upon). First is what I termed compassion joy (CJ), a unique type of enjoyment that feels good, is consciously felt, intrinsically rewarding, and to my knowledge, little studied to date. That this occurs needs documentation, not simply my suggestion, but if I am right, then efforts to cultivate global compassion should make use of the consequence of feeling good about having acted compassionately, motivating further compassionate behavior by providing the opportunity to so engage again and again.[p]

[p] My hunch is that CJ is a mild not a strong emotion, and hence, can be easily overwhelmed by the excitement obtained when defeating someone in a game or real life. It is also possible that in some people, those who devote themselves to global compassion, have a much stronger CJ response.

Quite separate is the enhancement of self-image that can occur from having acted compassionately. And still separate from that is the enhancement in how others regard the person who acts compassionately if what they do is known by others (see the footnote on page 23 for Harbaugh's earlier cited intrinsic and extrinsic rewards).

Recent research strongly suggests that there is an inborn predisposition to act compassionately. Very young children will attempt to console another child manifesting distress, even a child who is a stranger (for more on this, see the discussion in Paul Bloom's new book[9]). What happens to that predisposition so that it is not strengthened in most people, enabling global compassion in adolescents and adults? Answers to this question are found at the end of the excerpt from my most recent discussion with the Dalai Lama, in Chapter 7.

CHAPTER 6

Researchable Questions about Compassion

In this chapter, I both summarize researchable questions that I have already described about the nature of compassion and raise new questions that reach across the distinctions that I have drawn. The questions are organized by topic. Over one hundred researchable questions are described.

My goal in writing this account has not been to provide answers (for there are few), but to articulate at least some of the questions that can be and need to be answered. It is my fervent hope that this will stimulate or provoke students and colleagues to consider some or all of these questions, for I cannot, having closed my research laboratory when I retired nearly a decade ago.

Some readers might want to skip this chapter and turn to the Chapter 7, in which I discussed many of the ideas presented here with the Dalai Lama in the winter of 2012.

THE NATURE OF COMPASSION

Much earlier (pages 15–16), I distinguished between compassionate feelings, in which the compassionate person resonates to the feelings of the sufferer (empathic compassion), actions to relieve suffering (action compassion), and concern about another's suffering (concern compassion). Does action compassion always require first the experience of empathic compassion, or might action compassion be trained directly? Do you need to first feel the target's suffering before you can be motivated to act to relieve that suffering? Another question is whether a primary focus on training concern compassion results in more action compassion? Is one type of training more successful than another in increasing stranger compassion, or does it depend on the trainer, the trainee, and other circumstances?

Are compassionate actions always preceded by a conscious awareness of compassionate feelings? Might that be so for only some people, or all people? Is that order—feelings followed by actions—more prominent in familial than stranger compassion? Is it consistent within each individual but may differ in other persons? Might compassionate feelings less often precede compassionate actions when the compassion is distal and not proximal, with cognitive processes playing a more prominent role in distal than proximal compassion?

Compassion of any kind will not occur unless the compassionate person accurately recognizes that someone is suffering now or is likely to suffer in the future.

Do these two perceptions depend on very different psychological processes? Is the failure to act to prevent future suffering the consequence of different events, internal and external, than the failure to act to prevent or alleviate current suffering? For example, bad social forecasting or a belief that problems work themselves out or other such beliefs might justify a failure to act to prevent future suffering. Do the practices that focus on loving-kindness increase the likelihood of compassionate acts when the danger is in the future, not the present?

Are compassionately motivated acts to prevent future harm due solely to dispositional or situational factors or to the combination of the two? Developmental and longitudinal research is needed to determine this.

Is there a signal that distinguishes the occurrence of compassionate feelings and the different forms of resonance that result in compassionate actions? Are there signals that distinguish the occurrence of familial as compared to stranger compassion? What are the neurophysiological substrates that distinguish between compassionate feelings and the different forms of resonance described?

Does increasing independence of a family member decrease the compassion felt toward that family member?

Why is global compassion active from early life in some, but not most, people without some special event activating it? How can global compassion be increased? Are there certain life experiences that occur in most people who exhibit global compassion, pointing toward what is required to activate a genetic predisposition, if indeed there is such a predisposition in all people?

Is there an inborn predisposition to act compassionately in all or nearly all children? If so, why is it not strengthened and maintained in all or nearly all children, resulting in universal global compassion when they become adolescents and adults? Is it possible that mass media entertainment encountered in childhood and adolescence overwhelms and replaces compassionate impulses with the excitement of defeating an opponent and winning the game?

Is there any deficit in compassion among those who have been afflicted with PTSD?

RESONANCE

What is the difference, if any, between identical resonances felt by the observer witnessing the suffering of the person observed and the actual experience of the suffering person? Is there a difference between reactive resonance, which motivates attempts to relieve mental states other than suffering—for example, to reassure a fearful person or calm an angry person—and the identical compassion that motivates attempts to relieve an observed person's suffering? When suffering is observed, how can we explain whether identical resonance (feeling the other's suffering) or concern is experienced?

What is the difference in subjective feeling and in physiology when compassion is aimed at relieving what I earlier described as the second form of suffering, a malaise, and compassion aimed at relieving proximal suffering (the first type), in which the target is experiencing pain or some form of mental anguish?

What accounts for whether resonance that leads to compassionate actions is felt when suffering is observed? Are those who do not resonate to suffering more generally deficient in resonance to any observed emotion, or is the deficit more specific to suffering, and if so, is that a trait or more momentary phenomenon dependent on context, mood, etc.? Might people who do and do not act to relieve suffering have similar compassionate feelings but differ in risk taking or appraisal of the likelihood of risk? Or are such bystanders more generally indifferent to the suffering of others or perhaps to any emotion shown by others?

Do those who are not sympathetic to the suffering of others manifest a more general deficit in resonance? Is this the case in what has been described as burnout? Are people who experience burnout in their work setting indifferent to any emotion shown by any person, or is such a deficit more specific to a particular situation or a particular type of person? Or is it more emotion specific, for example, responsive to all emotions but not to suffering?

Are those who recognize more remote threats as emotionally aroused and motivated to act on those feelings, as is likely the case of those who act when recognizing the threat of immediate harm? Or might cognition play a stronger role than emotion in such instances?

Can resonance to observed suffering be taught, and if so, by what means? How does the success of an instructional method vary depending upon the age and other characteristics of the person being instructed or the context in which it is presented?

Is a disgust response to the physical manifestations of pain a stable, enduring personal characteristic, or might it be, in at least some people, an initial response soon followed by a more sympathetic form of resonance? Is concern for another person's suffering inextricably connected to a felt need to act to relieve that person's suffering?

While there has been emphasis on mother-infant attachment as responsible for the development of resonance and compassion, what role might the relationship among siblings and the relationship of the child to the father or other caregivers play? Is the concept of critical periods in a child's development relevant to understanding the development of resonance, familial, and other forms of compassion?

Do television viewers feel compassion toward those they see? What is the emotional experience of these people who seek to view suffering on television but take no action to relieve the suffering of the people they see or others. What is their motivation for watching these scenes of suffering?

RELATIONSHIPS AMONG DIFFERENT FORMS OF COMPASSION DISTINGUISHED BY TARGET

Is the strength of familial compassion related to the likelihood of stranger compassion? What accounts for individual differences, and how malleable are those differences in the scope and centrality of stranger compassion? Is familial compassion as intense and immediate for offspring, siblings, parents, cousins, uncles and aunts, or grandparents? Might the strength of familial compassion be determined not by genes shared but by the amount of intimate contact shared? Are the physiological changes that support familial compassion unique or similar to the physiological changes found in related emotions, such as sadness? Is there a context-free "snapshot"[q] signal for familial or other kinds of compassion?

Are compassionate feelings and/or actions an all-or-nothing matter or is there a gradient? Is the answer to that question dependent on whether one is considering familial, familiar, stranger, or sentient compassion; or does it instead depend on the individual, the context, etc.? If there are gradients, what is their shape, and what are the anchor points?

What, if any, are the commonalities in the self-reported explanations of why someone acted compassionately for familial, familiar, stranger, and the heroic subsets of each? Do they resemble each other in worldview, and if so, how early in life does worldview appear?

Is the strength of stranger compassion an inverse function of increasing differences in the genes shared

[q] The facial expressions of emotion that I have described and studied for seven emotions (anger, fear, sadness, disgust, contempt, surprise, and enjoyment) can be captured in a fraction of a second, a snapshot, and do not require observation of a sequence of changes in the face, head, or body.

between the observer and person observed? Adoption studies I expect would reveal that shared genes are not necessary for strong familial compassion, but I know of no studies of compassion in adoptive parents.

What role does formal secular or religious education play in the occurrence of familiar or stranger compassion and the heroic subsets of each? How common is religious faith mentioned in the self-reported explanations given by those who act compassionately, whether it is familiar, stranger, or the heroic variations of each? Is the strength of familiars compassion related to the extent of interdependence or shared critical experiences?

STRANGER COMPASSION

Why do some people manifest stranger compassion while most people do not, or at least do not organize their lives around a devotion to stranger compassion? Is it mere chance, not explicable in any known terms? Or might it be something in the upbringing of these people? Do some genetic factors predispose individuals to have stranger compassion?

Do cultures differ in the extent to which stranger compassion is found, in either the likelihood of it occurring at all, in the frequency with which it occurs across members of the culture, and in the scope or centrality of familial compassion? The same questions can be raised for other demographic characteristics: social class, education, male/female, etc. Buddhist scholar Alan Wallace has suggested that stranger compassion was the ideal in traditional Tibetan culture and found in a majority of the population. How has a concern with stranger compassion, present in all the Abrahamic religions today, varied historically?

Does the advent of televised presentations of stranger suffering in documentaries, news reports, and entertainment enhance or detract from the occurrence, scope, and centrality of stranger or heroic compassion? Does the impact vary with the demographic or other characteristics of the viewer, the narrative context in which the suffering occurs, and/or variations in childhood experience of being the recipient of familial compassion?

How widespread is toddler compassion that endures through childhood and adolescence? Does toddler compassion vary with upbringing, personality, or culture, or does it appear to be universal at an early age? Equally important would be to determine when this begins to disappear. Do the recent studies that children form in-group/out-group determinations as early as four years old[31] imply that consoling would become less prevalent toward those strange children recognized as out-group members? If a child is exposed early to other children of various demographic characteristics, would the in-group/out-group distinctions still emerge? At what age does stranger compassion become the exception rather than the rule? (The age at which this becomes evident and why this might be so remain to be determined.)

Which type of compassion training (concern compassion vs. action compassion) results in more trainees experiencing and acting upon stranger compassion?

For those involved in meditative practices, what might account for who responds to strangers and who does not? Do contemplative practices generate truly global compassion, toward strangers who differ in appearance, language, and culture? Are there extreme experiences that will turn on or turn off stranger compassion?

To what extent do demand characteristics explain the findings on the benefits of compassion training?

COMPASSION OVERLOAD: BURNOUT

My daughter, Eve Ekman, has contributed the following section:

> Humans are hardwired for an automatic emotional resonance with or contagion by the expressed emotions of others, especially intense negative emotions, such as pain and suffering.[62,63] The automatic emotional resonance with the suffering and pain of patients translates to a feeling of sympathetic distress.[59,62] This sympathetic distress, or any stress, can be functional at certain levels to rally our system to response; sympathetic distress can motivate empathic behavior, altruism, and engagement.[2,5,60] However, too much sympathetic distress can also be emotionally overwhelming, draining, and lead to empathic fatigue and feelings of burnout.[1,61,107]
>
> Our automatic emotional resonance was not designed with human service care providers in mind; from an

evolutionary perspective, the emotional response and concern for others' suffering is functional within small tribal groups where each individual's welfare is important to the group's survival.[20] Social rewards are built in to this small-group survival system: We naturally feel good about helping others, which provides a powerful intrinsic motivation to build on.[4] On the other hand, the everyday volume of suffering in a hospital setting, where there are not enough resources to meet the needs of all patients, requires building clear boundaries for concern. Without support to develop these clear boundaries, experiencing emotional resonance with the suffering of clients can develop into a paralyzing and persistent state of sympathetic distress.[23,32,xxii]

I believe Eve Ekman has raised a very important issue, with which I agree, about how modern arrangements for providing care for those who suffer, such as hospitals, can overload the emotion/compassion capacity of most, if not all, human beings unless corrective procedures are applied to prevent burnout. Just which corrective procedures are most effective for which caregivers is yet to be determined.

Do people who experience burnout of stranger compassion in the workplace recover and once again seek workplaces focused on stranger compassion? What accounts for why some people do and some people do not experience burnout of stranger compassion in their workplace, and if experienced, why some people recover and others do not?

HEROIC COMPASSION

Is heroic compassion shown by other animals? (pp. 105–107)[26] Does heroic compassion occur in all primates? And just in primates? In humans, heroic compassion is typically reported toward strangers, but it also occurs toward familiars, such as in small military groups. What distinguishes those who have heroic compassion toward familiars from other members of a small intensively acquainted group who do not experience or act heroically? Are those who experienced heroic compassion toward familiars likely to experience stranger compassion, either before or after their heroic acts?

Why do some, but not most, people show stranger and/or heroic compassion? What predicts who will act heroically toward strangers or familiars? Is nonheroic stranger compassion always a predictor of who is likely to act heroically when the situation demands it? In other words, what is the likelihood that a person who acts heroically never manifested nonheroic stranger compassion? What are the consequences of having acted with heroic compassion toward strangers or familiars on the heroic person's subsequent life? What are the consequences of not acting heroically when the situation demanded it?

If one member of a family has shown heroic compassion toward strangers, is it likely that it will be manifest in other family members? Is it more common in both identical twins than in both fraternal twins? Are there particular cultural backgrounds that generate a higher incidence of such heroic compassion? Are there any commonalities in the early experiences of those who later are heroically compassionate toward strangers? What are the characteristics of newly formed small groups that later produce someone who confronts danger to the group with heroism as compared to groups that confront danger without anyone acting heroically?

Is there evidence of a genetic predisposition for heroic compassion? If so, how might it be related to a possible genetic contribution to stranger compassion? Are there cultural, educational, and/or familial experiences in common among those who show heroic compassion?

Does PTSD extinguish or diminish compassionate feelings and actions?

COMPASSION JOY (CJ)

Is the experience of compassion enjoyment different in physiology, subjective experience, and appearance, from other enjoyable emotions? Is the experience the same when the compassion is proximal as compared to distal, familial, familiar, or stranger? Is what the Dalai Lama calls *rejoicing*, the enjoyment felt when witnessing someone who has acted compassionately, likely to motivate compassion in the person who has rejoiced; that is, does witnessing compassionate acts inspire compassionate acts in the witness; does it result in CJ?

Does CJ depend on whether the suffering was relieved by the compassionate person's actions? Does CJ motivate further compassionate behavior?

These are certainly not all the questions that can be raised by the distinctions I have drawn, but sufficient to underline the variety of fascinating, important issues that deserve exploration.

CHAPTER 7

Discussion with the Dalai Lama

I asked the Dalai Lama for the opportunity to discuss these ideas with him, and in January of 2012, we spent two days in New Delhi, India, considering many of the ideas described in the previous pages. An excerpt from that discussion follows.[r]

Ekman: *I feel a sense of urgency about global compassion. Time has run out. In the nineteenth century, you could read about the idea of interdependence, but you could live your own life, and the lives of other people did not impact on you. Now with climate change, with water shortage, with food shortage, it is really necessary to find commonalities.*

Dalai Lama: Right, right.

Ekman: *It is in that sense a Buddhist world. It wasn't so urgent a hundred years ago as it is now.*

---

[r] For access to the full discussion email info@paulekman.com.

Dalai Lama: The twentieth century became a century of violence. But also many wonderful things were invented. But then all those wonderful findings, scientific and technological inventions, quite often became the additional sources of destruction, sources of problems, sources of suffering. If such amount of suffering and bloodshed really brought the world into better shape, then there could be some justification for such immense violence. But that is not the case.

Even at the beginning of this century, some unhealthy things here and there, these certainly independently develop, but due to past mistakes, past negligence. So now, genuine peace, nonviolence ultimately live with our emotion, our mind. Now the teachings, preaching in the various religious traditions centuries old, more or less a little bit isolated, so not much influence on humanity in general.

So therefore, only effective way to provide some sort of change in our emotion is only through education, not through religious prayer. Now, how to introduce, how to bring moral education, education for ethics, into modern education system. If we rely on religious belief or faith, then what religion? There are many religious beliefs. Some say God, some say no God.

So the conclusion is very easy. We must find ways and means to cultivate warm-heartedness without touching religion, using our common sense, and using many areas of common sense. Now here, the scientific finding is very, very suitable, the importance of element to bring conviction to people. And also there is the secular, of course.... The basic sort of aim is how to cultivate calm mind. With calm mind, our intelligence also can be utilized properly. With a disturbed mind, we cannot utilize our intelligence properly. It cannot see positively. So calm mind is very, very important.

Then how to develop calm mind? The destroyers of calm mind are anger, hatred, fear, suspicion, distrust—these things. So therefore, the opposite, counterforce of these things is warm-heartedness: respect others, love others, recognize their rights. Then there is no room for anger, no room for hatred, no room for fear. If someone gives love to others, then most probably the others at least also will give some kind of feeling of safety. Maybe their response will not be equal response, but at least their fear, their anger will be reduced; their suspicion will be reduced. So, the method to create calm mind. Then the subject of compassion.

I felt at the beginning in order to cultivate warm-heartedness, in order to educate about warm-heartedness . . . I felt firstly should have some knowledge about the map of emotions, about the relations between different emotions and contradictory forces. Once you get a more clearer picture, like a map, then if you want to reach that, you have to go through that way, not through meditation and expect that suddenly something will change. Not that way. Like in ancient time, in order to go someplace like America, you had to create a map to go from here and there. Similarly, when we talk about calm mind, not through prayer, not through miracle, we have to know what is the seed of calm mind, what is the destroyer of calm mind, the seed of the destroyer; you should have some knowledge about the world of emotions. Then the way of training of compassion and warm-heartedness, starting with the family and then to global compassion. . . . So, on the basis of your work with facial expressions, I would like to develop an updated dictionary of emotions.

Ekman: *I am glad to hear you believe that it will be helpful for people if they understand their emotions and don't just push them aside. But understand their emotions well enough so that their emotions can work for them and develop a warm-hearted attitude.*[s]

Dalai Lama: In order to train genuine compassion, you should practice detachment. Why? So long as your sense of concern for another's well-being is mixed with attachment, that always becomes biased. And also, you see that always very much based on another's attitude.

Even mother, who is very, very kind to you—you have a special sort of feeling of closeness. If your mother does not care for you, even though your physical body was given by that person, but still you do not feel much. That kind of compassion is very much based on others' attitudes. That kind of compassion is impossible to extend towards your enemy who actually harming on you. So now that kind of compassion, that sense of concern, that sense of closeness of feeling is very

[s] I had to postpone working on the map of emotions the Dalai Lama called for in our discussion, and reportedly continues to request in his public speeches, until I finished this manuscript. I have just begun the mapping work.

much based on emotion or attachment. That must be reduced in order to develop an unbiased sense of concern or unbiased compassion. Unbiased compassion is not oriented towards another's attitude but to the other being itself.

Just like attachment or feeling love for oneself; it is not based on your own attitude towards yourself. Simply, I want happiness. I do not want suffering. On that basis, there is desire to overcome suffering. Therefore, there is a sense of concern for your own suffering. Similarly, others not thinking of their attitude toward you; they are indifferent what their attitude toward you. But they also, like me, they do not want suffering, so they have every right to overcome suffering.

On that level, they develop some sense of concern for their well-being. Now not oriented on their attitude, but based on their recognition, they also have—just like me—they have a right to overcome their own suffering. No difference if it is your relative, your enemy, or stranger, or solo sentient being, solo human being. All want to overcome suffering. On the basis of that kind of understanding, they develop a sense of concern—that is genuine compassion, unbiased.

Ekman: *Unbiased in the sense that it is uninfluenced by the nature of that other person's attitude or behavior, I presume?*

Dalai Lama: This is mine. This is our friend. That is biased. This is my friend. This is our friend. Automatically our enemy. On the humanity level, there is no basis for demarcation as friend or enemy.

Ekman: *Where that does not work for me, if you feel stranger or global compassion, you are concerned about the suffering of anyone, and you do not know anything about that person. So you can't be biased by what you know about him or her. It is there simply because he or she is a human being. When you ask people who jump into the subway track, putting their own life at risk to rescue a stranger, why did you do it? They say, "Well, I had to do it. It is another person." That is unbiased.*

Dalai Lama: Yes, that is unbiased.

Ekman: *It is unbiased, because you do not have the chance to be biased. It is unbiased because you do not have the opportunity to be biased because you do not know anything about them.*

Dalai Lama: Oh yes. However, the compassion unbiased or unconditional compassion. The seed of that is biased compassion. My mother. My friend. That kind of compassion is the seed. Then, without that, the unbiased, unconditional compassion cannot develop. The seed of biased compassion must be there. Then take that seed, then use human intelligence, a type of human intelligence, then that level of biased compassion, then we have intelligence becoming unbiased, unconditional compassion. That is my way of approach.

Ekman: *It seems to me, there are two types of compassion: (1) proximal, when you are dealing with someone right at this moment, and (2) distal. And proximal is much more related to the emotions, and distal, to thinking and social forecasting.*

Dalai Lama: In Buddhism there is a very similar concept. One is feeling compassionate towards the other person, seeing the immediate suffering. The other one is seeing the causal conditions being gathered by the person, which would put the person into suffering in the future. At the moment, there is no experience of suffering. Now here, intelligence . . .

Ekman: *Intelligence plays the biggest role.*

Dalai Lama: The first step is to be able to educate people to see the downside [of] a completely individualistic rather than a global concern. To recognize the pros and cons, the benefits and disadvantages of compassion for all living beings. Narrow-mindedness, to think of one's own nation, one's own country, one's own tract, or only the West, America, and Europe, not thinking about Africa, Latin America, the Middle East, or Asia. So what is the benefit of that? First, to think globally is a positive benefit. The economy, the environment, and also the political system . . . I think of politics there is, how you say? Rivalry.

Ekman: *So what you are saying is that distal compassion that is focused on preventing suffering involves wisdom and knowledge and is accessible through teaching. Because it is based on thought, its absence is based on narrow-mindedness. Proximal compassion, such as "I hope you are not hurting as you are hurting right now." That kind of compassion is based on emotion, and it is immediate.*

Dalai Lama: I think if you take care of some others, hoping that later they help you, that is selfish. If I do selfish work and get a good name. I become more popular. All that is selfish.

Ekman: *You put your name on the hospital, you donate the hospital, and it is the "Dalai Lama Hospital."*

Dalai Lama: From a Buddhist perspective, this is known as one of the "worldly concerns."

Ekman: *So if you reject that, but clearly much of gift-giving, much of the good things that go on in the world that save people from starving or dying without treatment are from people who do it either to wish that someone will do it back to them, or more likely, so that people will know their name and think, "Aren't they a wonderful person?" Now everybody benefits. No question. Huge benefits. We do not necessarily want to stop people from doing that. Better that than buying fancy cars. If you reject that as the motivation for distal [compassion], what is the motivation?*

Dalai Lama: I think a genuine sense of concern for others' well-being should not involve your own interest.

[*The Dalai Lama then initiated a long discussion with Geshe Dorji Damdul, an advisor as well as translator. What follows is Damdul's summary of their discussion.*]

Geshe Dorji Damdul: From a Buddhist perspective, there is the concept of the Bodhisattva ideal: someone who wishes, engages in all virtuous actions, such as generosity and so forth, with the objective to become a Buddha himself. But then His Holiness is wondering if that action of generosity is purely for others, or is it mixed with personal interest, which is to become a Buddha yourself. In one Buddhist text it is mentioned that you should be courageous enough even to give your Buddhahood for others, even to make yourself accessible, everything that is within your capabilities be made accessible to others. This is known as wishing for Buddhahood; it is not for personal gain.

Ekman: *I understand what you just told me on an intellectual level, and I do not understand it at all beyond that.*

Dalai Lama: [*laughs*]

[*The next excerpt is from a few hours later in our conversation.*]

Dalai Lama: So years, years sort of some practice or training, through effort you develop strong sense of concern for others well-being that while you sort of meditate or thinking after a few minutes or several minutes. Then you get real sort of experience, that's experience through effort. After that, still practice continuously, then spontaneous sort of experience whenever you face something. Without the reasoning, without effort, effortlessly develop, that's the second state. Once that sort of experience, then no need for thought, something happens, response immediately comes.

[*Note the Dalai Lama has described two stages of developing compassion; the first takes effort, but if one reaches the second state, compassion just happens; it is part of you, not requiring special effort.*]

Ekman: *Recall the findings I mentioned earlier in our discussion, that very young children will, without encouragement or training, act to console another child they do not know, who is in distress.*

It appears that young children are inclined to be compassionate without training. This inclination is not strengthened by most of the entertainment media they are exposed to over the next years of their lives, the television programs, games, comic books, etc. The emphasis is on competition, not collaboration; on winning, not helping; on aggressive, not compassionate behavior. Such entertainment would not exist if it were not entertaining, enjoyable, to the children, adolescents, and adults who engage with it. Just as helping others feels good intrinsically, defeating others, winning the contest also feels good. While what is called prosocial entertainment does exist, it is not as prevalent and likely not as influential in the development of most children.

The world needs a prosocial global compassion entertainment array, which involves everything from toys to games, television programs to movies. It will be just as entertaining. It could be just as profitable, but it will start strengthening at this very impressionable age the virtue of doing good.

The heroes and heroines in these entertainments should inspire the viewer because of all the people they help and save, not because of all the people they kill. We must begin with the children, the world's children. If you, the Dalai Lama, are enthusiastic about creating such entertainments that encourage compassion, it will have an impact on the people who have the talent and the money to make it happen.

Dalai Lama: Must happen. No question.

Ekman: *Let me return to an idea I described yesterday, prefacing what I am about to describe by warning you I am speculating, basing what I say on my own experience and conversations with a few people, not scientific data. So here is the very simple, unproven assertion: when you do good, it feels good. When you act compassionately, even if no one knows that you did so, it makes you feel good.*

Dalai Lama: Yes!

Ekman: *It's like having a nice chocolate. You don't have to learn that it's a good thing to do.*

Dalai Lama: Do you like chocolate?

Ekman: *I like chocolate, yes.* [laughs] *Do you like chocolate?*

Dalai Lama: Last year, Mayo Clinic, I asked specifically physician, some people say chocolate is bad, some say good. I ask. They say OK. Since then, I got some liberation. [*laughs*]

Ekman: *There are many separate levels of benefit for a compassionate act. The most important one is the one that nature has built in. Nature did not just build in to the parent the need to protect and care for the child. It built into every living being that if you act in a selfless way to help others, it's going to be like a breath of fresh air.*

It's going to make you feel very good for a few moments. That's a wonderful thing.

Dalai Lama: Wonderful, yes. Absolutely.

Ekman: *It is intrinsically rewarding. For some people, it is even more rewarding to act compassionately anonymously, so nobody knows what you've done except for you. For some people, that is the sweetest of all.*

Dalai Lama: That's right, that's right.

Ekman: *Acting to help other people makes us feel good. That is a building block that is there in the four-year-old, and we need to strengthen it. We want it to become the organizing principle of their life. It's not that we have to plant it, we only have to nourish it.*

Dalai Lama: That's right; if there's potential, then make effort nurturing.

Ekman: *We should start early.*

Dalai Lama: Yes. Absolutely

Ekman: *Four or five years old. It is likely at that age they're more receptive than any other age.*

Dalai Lama: I also believe at that age the nature, the potential, still most alive. That's my view, more sort of intelligence, more education, more experience.

Ekman: *It's extremely important how this kind of an effort is sponsored so it is seen not as promoting one nation, one religion, one viewpoint, but humanity. There will need to be planning by people more sophisticated* *than I am as to how to do that. But I think we are at a critical juncture because I think the opportunity is there, the technology is there, the need is there, and we are at a tipping point. You know this concept of the tipping point?*

Dalai Lama: Yes. So then as far as I know, some sort of professors, some sort of universities already carry some kind of educational program in schools as experiment. . . . Once we develop concrete curriculum, then start one school, test, then watch . . . then other school, then eventually global level.

Ekman: *A different approach than you are proposing, but with the same goal: Children spend a lot of time out of school, playing games, watching television. We don't have to get the approval from a board of education or a teacher. We just have to generate the materials, and if those materials are attractive and fun, then children will want them, parents will get them, and the kids will start using them. Some of it may drift into the classroom, but at least in America, getting something into the classroom can take years of bureaucracies with school boards and all of that. It's a much faster, easier route, if the kids want it, and if they enjoy it, and if the television companies find, "Oh, these kids watch this program," it will happen. It may be an easier route than the schools.*

Entertainment can be the cover for education. You have to enjoy it. The United States is a master of the technology of entertainment. I'm afraid if you go through the school route, you'll get trapped by the bureaucracies and the competiveness and that could slow everything down or strangle it.

Dalai Lama: That's your responsibility not mine, how to approach this. [*laughs*] You should explore.

Ekman: *I will explore if I have your backing.*

Dalai Lama: Yes. Full support. [*laughs*] Full support. I have order with you. And when I visit with the United States, can we make some sort of program.

Ekman: *Yes.*

Dalai Lama: I'm ready.

Ekman: *That's good.*

FINAL NOTE

Follow-up on the issues raised in the last part of our discussion was delayed a year and a half by a series of health crises that afflicted me. Now it is my hope that by making this book available and sending it to a few media people I came to know when working as a consultant on the national entertainment TV program *Lie to Me*, that interest will be stimulated. I may be naïve to think that there will be commercial interest in developing entertainments that strengthen CJ, through collaboration, cooperation, joint problem solving, and so forth. I will find out.

My next task, which I have just begun, is to work on the map of emotions the Dalai Lama has called for.

POSTSCRIPT

"We have the capacity to think several centuries into the future. Start the task, even if it will not be fulfilled in your lifetime. This generation has a responsibility to reshape the world. . . . We must ask ourselves about how we lead our life, in the service of what exactly are we using whatever talents we may have? . . . To check our motivation, we must ask:

Is it just for me, or for others?

For the benefit of the few, or the many?

For now, or for the future?"

—These quotes from the Dalai Lama are from the last pages of Daniel Goleman's new book *Focus*.[53]

"The moral sense, or conscience, is as much a part of man as his leg or arm. It is given to all human beings in a stronger or weaker degree, as force of members is given them in a greater or lesser degree. It may be strengthened by exercise, as may any particular limb of the body."

—This quote from Thomas Jefferson, 1787, is from the front of Paul Bloom's new book, *Just Babies.*[9]

REFERENCES

1. Ashforth, B. (1994). Petty tyranny in organizations. *Human Relations, 47(7)*, 755-778. doi:10.1177/001872679404700701

2. Baron-Cohen, S. (2011). *The science of evil: On empathy and the origins of cruelty.* New York, NY: Basic Books.

3. Batson, C. D. (2011). *Altruism in humans.* New York, NY: Oxford University Press.

4. Batson, C. D., Batson, J. G., Slingsby, J. K., Harrell, K. L., Peekna, H. M., & Todd, R. M. (1991). Empathic joy and the empathy-altruism hypothesis. *Journal of Personality and Social Psychology, 61(3)*, 413-426.

5. Batson, C. D., Lishner, D. A., Cook, J., & Sawyer, S. (2005). Similarity and nurturance: Two possible sources of empathy for strangers. *Basic and Applied Social Psychology, 27(1)*, 15-25.

6. Baumann, D. J., Cialdini, R. B., & Kendrick, D. T. (1981). Altruism as hedonism: Helping and self-gratification as equivalent responses. *Journal of Personality and Social Psychology, 40*, 1039-1046.

7. Belin, P., Fillion-Bilodeau, S., & Gosselin, F. (2008). The Montreal Affective Voices: A validated set of nonverbal affect bursts for research on auditory affective processing. *Behavior Research Methods, 40*, 531-539.

8. Blau, K., Franco, Z., & Zimbardo, P. (2009). Fostering the heroic imagination: An ancient ideal and a modern vision. *Eye on Psi Chi, 13*, 18-21.

9. Bloom, P. (2013). *Just babies: The origins of good and evil.* New York, NY: Crown Publishing Group.

10. Boucher, J. D. & Ekman, P. (1975). Facial areas and emotional information. *Journal of Communication, 25(2),* 21–29.

11. Brownell, C. (2013). Early development of prosocial behavior: Current perspectives. *Infancy, 18(1),* 1–9. doi:10.1111/infa.12004

12. Carlo, G., Eisenberg, N., Troyer, D., Switzer, G., & Speer, A. L. (1991). The altruistic personality: In what contexts is it apparent? *Journal of Personality and Social Psychology, 61(3),* 450–458.

13. Condon, P., Desbordes, G., Miller, W. B., & DeSteno, D. (2013). Meditation increases compassionate responses to suffering. *Psychological Science, 24(10),* 2125–2127.

14. Craig, K. D., Hyde, S. A., & Patrick, C. J. (1997). Genuine, suppressed, and faked facial behavior during exacerbation of chronic low back pain. In Ekman, P., & Rosenberg, E. L. (Eds.), *What the face reveals* (pp. 161–180). New York, NY: Oxford University Press.

15. Crawford, C. & Krebs, D. (Eds.). (2008). *Foundations of evolutionary psychology.* New York, NY: Taylor & Francis Group.

16. Cutler, H. C. & Dalai Lama. (1998). *The art of happiness: A handbook for living.* New York, NY: Riverhead Books.

17. Dalai Lama & Ekman, P. (2008). *Emotional awareness: Overcoming the obstacles to psychological balance and compassion: A conversation between the Dalai Lama and Paul Ekman.* New York, NY: Times Books/Henry Holt.

18. Darwin, C. (1871). *The descent of man, and selection in relation to sex.* New York, NY: D. Appleton.

19. Darwin, C. (1872). *The expression of the emotions in man and animals.* London, UK: John Murray, Albemarle Street.

20. Darwin, C. (1936). *The origin of species by means of natural selection: Or the preservation of favored races in the struggle for life, and the descent of man and selection in relation to sex.* New York, NY: Modern Library.

21. Darwin, C. (1998). *The expression of the emotions in man and animals* (3rd ed.). Ekman, P. (Ed.). New York, NY: Oxford University Press. (Second edition published 1879)

22. Darwin, C. (2004). *The descent of man, and selection in relation to sex.* Moore, J., & Desmond, A. (Eds.). London, UK: Penguin Books. (Original work published 1871)

23. Davis, M. H. (1983). Measuring individual differences in empathy: Evidence for a multidimensional approach. *Journal of Personality and Social Psychology, 44(1),* 113-126.

24. Davis, M. H. (1996). *Empathy: A social psychological approach.* Boulder, CO: Westview Press.

25. De Drue, C. K. W. (2012). Oxytocin modulates cooperation within and competition between groups: An Integrative review and research agenda. *Hormones and Behavior, 61(3),* 419-428. doi:10.1016/j.yhbeh.2011.12.009

26. de Waal, F. (2009). *The age of empathy: Nature's lessons for a kinder society.* New York, NY: Crown Publishing Group.

27. de Waal, F. B. M. (2008). Putting the altruism back into altruism: The evolution of empathy. *Annual Review of Psychology, 59,* 279-300.

28. Decety, J. (2011). Dissecting the neural mechanisms mediating empathy. *Emotion Review, 3(1),* 92-108.

29. Decety, J. & Jackson, P. L. (2004). The functional architecture of human empathy. *Behavioral Cognitive Neuroscience Review, 3,* 71-100.

30. Dimberg, U., Andréasson, P., & Thunberg, M. (2011). Emotional empathy and facial reactions to facial expressions. *Journal of Psychophysiology, 25(1),* 26-31.

31. Dunham, Y., Chen, E. E., & Banaji, M. R. (2013). Two Signatures of implicit intergroup attitudes: Developmental invariance and early enculturation. *Psychological Science, 24(6),* 860-868. doi:10.1177/0956797612463081

32. Eisenberg, N. (2000). Emotion, regulation and moral development. *Annual Review of Psychology, 51,* 665-697.

33. Eisenberg, N. & Fabes, R. A. (1990). Empathy: Conceptualization, measurement, and relation to prosocial behavior. *Motivation and Emotion, 14(2),* 131-149.

34. Eisenberg, N., Fabes, R. A., Guthrie, I. K., & Reiser, M. (2000). Dispositional emotionality and regulation: Their role in predicting quality of social functioning. *Journal of Personality and Social Psychology, 78(1),* 136-157. doi:10.1037/0022-3514.78.1.136

35. Eisenberg, N., Fabes, R. A., Murphy, B., Karbon, M., Maszk, P., Smith, M., . . . Suh, K. (1994). The relations of emotionality and regulation to dispositional and situational empathy-related responding. *Journal of Personality and Social Psychology, 66(4),* 776–797.

36. Ekman, E. & Halpern, J. (in review). Professional distress and well-being among human service care providers: Professional empathy can help.

37. Ekman, P. (1972). Universals and cultural differences in facial expressions of emotion. In Cole, J. (Ed.), *Nebraska symposium on motivation* (pp. 207–283). Lincoln, NE: University of Nebraska Press, 1972.

38. Ekman, P. (1989). The argument and evidence about universals in facial expression of emotion. In Manstead, A., & Wagner, H. (Eds.), *Handbook of social psychophysiology* (pp. 143–164). Chichester, UK: John Wiley & Sons.

39. Ekman, P. (1993). Facial expression and emotion. *American Psychologist, 48,* 384–392.

40. Ekman, P. (1999). Facial expressions. In Dagleish, T., & Power, T. (Eds.), *The handbook of cognition and emotion* (pp. 301–320). Sussex, UK: John Wiley & Sons, Ltd.

41. Ekman, P. (2003). *Emotions revealed: Recognizing faces and feelings to improve communication and emotional life.* New York, NY: Time Books.

42. Ekman, P. (2010). Darwin's compassionate view of human nature. *JAMA: Journal of the American Medical Association, 303,* 557–558.

43. Ekman, P. & Cordaro, D. (in review). Darwin's proposal that facial expressions of emotion are universal is not challenged.

44. Ekman, P. & Davidson, R. J. (1994). Affective science: A research agenda. In Ekman, P., & Davidson, R. J. (Eds.), *The nature of emotion: Fundamental questions* (pp. 411–430). New York, NY: Oxford University Press.

45. Ekman, P. & Friesen, W. V. (1975). *Unmasking the face: A guide to recognizing emotions from facial clues.* Upper Saddle River, NJ: Prentice Hall.

46. Etcoff, N. L., Ekman, P., Magee, J. J., & Frank, M. G. (2000). Lie detection and language comprehension. *Nature, 405,* 139. doi:10.1038/35012129

47. Franco, Z. E., Blau, K., & Zimbardo, P. G. (2011). Heroism: A conceptual analysis and differentiation between heroic action and altruism. *Review of General Psychology, 15(2),* 99–113.

48. Franco, Z. & Zimbardo, P. (2007; Fall–Winter). The Banality of Heroism. *Greater Good,* 30–35.

49. Galen, L. W. (2012). Does religious belief promote prosociality? A critical examination. *Psychological Bulletin, 138(5),* 876–906. doi:10.1037/a0028251

50. Gilbert, P. & Tirch, D. (2009). Emotional memory, mindfulness and compassion. In Gilbert, P., & Tirch, D., *Clinical handbook of mindfulness* (p. 99–110). New York, NY: Springer Science + Business Media.

51. Goetz, J., Keltner, D., & Simon-Thomas, E. (2010). Compassion: An evolutionary analysis and empirical review. *Psychological Bulletin, 136,* 351–374.

52. Goleman, D. (2006). *Social intelligence: The new science of human relationships.* New York, NY: Bantam Books.

53. Goleman, D. (2013). *Focus: The hidden driver of excellence.* New York, NY: Harper Collins.

54. Greenberg, L. (1979). Genetic component of bee odor in kin recognition. *Science,* 206, 1095–1097.

55. Gyurak, A., Haase, C. M., Sze, J., Goodkind, M. S., Coppola, G., Lane, J., Levenson, R. W. (2013). The effect of the serotonin transporter polymorphism (5-HTTLPR) on empathic and self-conscious emotional reactivity. *Emotion, 13(1),* 25–35. doi:10.1037/a0029616

56. Hamilton, W. D. (1964). The genetical evolution of social behaviour I. *Journal of Theoretical Biology,* 7, 1–16. doi.org/10.1016/0022-5193(64)90038-4

57. Harbaugh, W. T. (1998). The prestige motive for making charitable transfers. *American Economic Review, 88(2),* 277–282.

58. Hatfield, E., Cacioppo, J. T., & Rapson, R. L. (1993). Emotional contagion. *Current Directions in Psychological Science, 2,* 96–99.

59. Hatfield, E. & Rapson, R. L. (1998). Emotional contagion. *Progress in Communication Sciences, 14*, 73–89.

60. Hein, G. & Singer, T. (2008). I feel how you feel but not always: The empathic brain and its modulation. *Cognitive Neuroscience, 18(2)*, 153–158. doi:10.1016/j.conb.2008.07.012

61. Hoschild, A. (1983). *The managed heart: The commercialization of human feeling*. Berkeley, CA: University of California Press. Reprinted with new afterword in 2003.

62. Iacoboni, M. (2009). Imitation, empathy, and mirror neurons. *Annual Review of Psychology, 60*, 653–670. doi:10.1146/annurev.psych.60.110707.163604

63. Ickes, W., Funder, D. C., & West, S. G. (1993). Empathic accuracy. *Journal of Personality, 61(4)*, 587–610.

64. Ickes, W. & Simpson, J. A. (1997). Managing empathic accuracy in close relationships. In Ickes, W., & Simpson, J. A., *Empathic accuracy* (pp. 218–250). New York, NY: Guilford Press.

65. Jacobs, T. L., Epel, E. S., Lin, J., Blackburn, E. H., Wolkowitz, O. M., Bridwell, D. A., . . . Saron, C. D. (2011). Intensive meditation training, immune cell telomerase activity, and psychological mediators. *Psychoneuroendocrinology, 36(5)*, 664–681.

66. Keltner, D., Ekman, P., Gonzaga, G. C., & Beer, J. (2003). Facial expression of emotion. In Davidson, R. J., Scherer, K. R., & Goldsmith, H. H. (Eds.), *Handbook of affective sciences*. New York, NY: Oxford University Press.

67. Keltner, D. & Harker, L. (1998). The forms and functions of the nonverbal signal of shame. In Keltner, D., & Harker, L., *Shame: Interpersonal behavior, psychopathology, and culture* (pp. 78–98). New York, NY: Oxford University Press.

68. Kemeny, M. E., Foltz, C., Cavanagh, J. F., Cullen, M., Giese-Davis, J., Jennings, P., . . . Ekman, P. (2011). Contemplative/emotion training reduces negative emotional behavior and promotes prosocial response. *Emotion, 12(2)*, 338–350. doi:10.1037/a0026118

69. Klimecki, O. M., Leiberg, S., Lamm, C., & Singer, T. (2013). Functional neural plasticity and associated changes in positive affect after compassion training. *Cerebral Cortex, 23*, 1552–1561.

70. Klimecki, O. M., Leiberg, S., Ricard, M., & Singer, T. (2013). Differential pattern of functional brain plasticity after compassion and empathy training. *Social Cognitive and Affective Neuroscience Advance Access*. doi:10.1093/scan/nst060

71. Knafo, A., Zahn-Waxler, C., Van Hulle, C., Robinson, J. L., & Rhee, S. H. (2008). The developmental origins of a disposition toward empathy: Genetic and environmental contributions. *Emotion, 8(6)*, 737–752. doi:10.1037/a0014179

72. LeDoux, J. (1998). *The emotional brain: The mysterious underpinnings of emotional life*. New York, NY: Simon & Schuster.

73. Levenson, R. & Ruef, A. (1992). Empathy: A physiological substrate. *Journal of Personality and Social Psychology, 63*, 234–246.

74. Levine, R. (2012). The kindness of strangers [PowerPoint slides]. Presentation at the Science of Compassion Conference in Telluride, CO.

75. Levine, R. V. (2003). The kindness of strangers. *American Scientist, 91*, 226–233.

76. Lockwood, P., Millings, A., Hepper, E., & Rowe, A. C. (2013). If I cry, do you care? Individual differences in empathy moderate the facilitation of caregiving words after exposure to crying faces. *Journal of Individual Differences, 34(1)*, 41–47. doi:10.1027/1614-0001/a000098

77. MacLean, K. A., Ferrer, E., Aichele, S. R., Bridwell, D. A., Zanesco , A. P., Jacobs, T., Saron, C. D. (2010). Intensive meditation training improves perceptual discrimination and sustained attention. *Psychological Science, 21(6)*, 829–839. doi:10.1177/0956797610371339

78. Manning, R., Levine, M., & Collins, A. (2007). The Kitty Genovese murder and the social psychology of helping: The parable of the 38 witnesses. *American Psychologist, 62*, 555–562.

79. Mascaro, J. S., Rilling, J. K., Negi, L. T., & Raison, C. L. (2012). Compassion meditation enhances empathic accuracy and related neural activity. *Social Cognitive and Affective Neuroscience, 8*, 48–55. doi:10.1093/scan/nss095

80. Maslach, C. & Leiter, M. P. (2008). Early predictors of job burnout and engagement. *Journal of Applied Psychology, 93(3)*, 498–512.

81. Miller, R. E., Caul, W. F., & Mirsky, I. A. (1967). Communication of affects between feral and socially isolated monkeys. *Journal of Personality and Social Psychology, 7(3),* 231–239. doi:10.1037/h0025065

82. Moll, J., Krueger, F., Zahn, R., Pardini, M., de Oliveira-Souza, R., & Grafman, J. (2006). Human fronto-mesolimbic networks guide decisions about charitable donation. *PNAS, 103(42),* 15623–15628. doi:10.1073/pnas.0604475103

83. Monroe, K. R. (1996). *The heart of altruism.* Princeton, NJ: Princeton University Press.

84. Monroe, K. R. (2004). *The hand of compassion: Portraits of moral choice during the holocaust.* Princeton, NJ: Princeton University Press.

85. Moore, J. & Desmond, A. (2004). Introduction. In Darwin, C., *The descent of man, and selection in relation to sex* (pp. xi–lviii). London, UK: Penguin Books. (Original work published 1871)

86. Preston, S. D. (2013). The origins of altruism in offspring care. *Psychological Bulletin.* doi:10.1037/a0031755

87. Preston, S. D. & de Waal, F. B. M. (2002). Empathy: Its ultimate and proximate bases. *Behavioral and Brain Sciences, 25,* 1–20.

88. Prkachin, K. M. (1997). The consistency of facial expressions of pain: A comparison across modalities. In Ekman, P., & Rosenberg, E. L. (Eds.), *What the face reveals* (pp. 181–200). New York, NY: Oxford University Press.

89. Rinpoche, P. (2011). *Words of my perfect teacher.* (Padmakara Translation Group, Trans.). New Haven & London: Yale University Press. (Original work published 1994)

90. Rosenberg, E. L., Zanesco, A. P., King, B. G., Aichele, S. R., Jacobs, T. L., Bridwell, D. A., . . . Saron, C. D. (in review). Training prosocial emotional responses to suffering: Facial and subjective indicators of engaged concern.

91. Roth-Hanania, R., Davidov, M., & Zahn-Waxler, C. (2011). Empathy development from 8 to 16 months: Early signs of concern for others. *Infant Behavior and Development, 34(3),* 447–458. doi:10.1016/j.infbeh.2011.04.007

92. Russell, A. T. (1994). The clinical presentation of childhood-onset schizophrenia. *Schizophrenia Bulletin, 20(4),* 631–646.

93. Sahdra, B. K., MacLean, K. A., Shaver, P. R., Ferrer, E., Rosenberg, E. L., Jacobs, T. L., . . . Saron, C. D. (2011). Enhanced response inhibition during intensive meditation training predicts improvements in self-reported adaptive socioemotional functioning. *Emotion, 11(2),* 299–312.

94. Saslow, L. R., John, O. P., Piff, P. K., Willer, R., Wong, E., Impett, E. A., . . . Saturn, S. R. (2013). The social significance of spirituality: New perspectives on the compassion-altruism relationship. *Psychology of Religion and Spirituality.* doi:10.1037/a0031870

95. Schuster, G., Smits, W., & Ullal, J. (2008). *Thinkers of the jungle: The orangutan report.* Königswinter, Germany: H.F. Ullmann.

96. Simon-Thomas, E. R., Keltner, D. J., Sauter, D., Sinicropi-Yao, L., & Abramson, A. (2009). The voice conveys specific emotions: Evidence from vocal burst displays. *Emotion, 9(6),* 838–846. doi:10.1037/a0017810

97. Simpson, B. & Willer, R. (2008). Altruism and indirect reciprocity: The interaction of person and situation in prosocial behavior. *Social Psychology Quarterly, 71,* 37–52.

98. Trivers, R. L. (1971). The evolution of reciprocal altruism. *Quarterly Review of Biology, 46,* 35–57. doi:10.1086/406755

99. van Kleef, G. A., Oveis, C., van der Löwe, I., LuoKogan, A., Goetz, J., & Keltner, D. (2008). Power, distress, and compassion: Turning a blind eye to the suffering of others. *Psychological Science, 19(12),* 1315–1322. doi:10.1111/j.1467-9280.2008.02241.x

100. Wallace, B. A. (2005). *Genuine happiness: Meditation as the path to fulfillment.* Hoboken, NJ: John Wiley & Sons.

101. Wallace, B. A. (2009). *Mind in the balance: Meditation in science, Buddhism, and Christianity.* New York, NY: Columbia University Press.

102. Warneken, F. & Tomasello, M. (2006). Altruistic helping in human infants and young chimpanzees. *Science, 311,* 1301–1303. doi:10.1126/science.1121448

103. Weng, H. Y., Fox, A. S., Shackman, A. J., Stodola, D. E., Caldwell, J. Z. K., Olson, M. C., . . . Davidson, R. J. (2013). Compassion training alters altruism and neural responses to suffering. *Psychological Science, 24(7),* 1171–1180. doi:10.1177/0956797612469537

104. Whitehouse, W. G., Orne, E. C., & Dinges, D. F. (2002). Demand characteristics: Toward an understanding of their meaning and application in clinical practice. *Prevention and Treatment, 5(1).* doi:10.1037/1522-3736.5.1.534i

105. Willer, R. (2009). Groups reward individual sacrifice: The status solution to the collective action problem. *American Sociological Review. 74,* 23–43.

106. Wolsko, P. M., Eisenberg, D. M., Davis, R. B., & Phillips, R. S. (2004). Use of mind-body medical therapies: Results of a national survey. *Journal of General Internal Medicine, 19(1),* 43–50.

107. Zammuner, V. L., Lotto, L., & Galli, C. (2003). Regulation of emotions in the helping professions: Nature, antecedents and consequences. *Australian e-Journal for the Advancement of Mental Health (AeJAMH), 2(1),* 1–13.

ENDNOTES

i I am grateful to the following people for their review and feedback about earlier versions of this book: Richard J. Davidson, Eve V. Ekman, Paul Kaufman, Erika Rosenberg, Clifford Saron, Alan Wallace (page 13).

ii I thank both my daughter Eve Ekman and Alan Wallace for bringing this to my attention (page 16).

iii See Monroe's[83] discussion of moral obligation (page 19).

iv Ekman & Friesen[45] and Ekman[40] described sadness as a resigned form of distress or suffering. After Boucher and Ekman[10] found that the term *distress* did not differentiate among physical pain, psychological suffering, or sadness, Ekman & Friesen utilized only the term *sadness* in their cross-cultural and other research on facial expression. Ekman later[41] proposed the term *anguish* for the more active or agitated version of this emotion, reserving the term *sadness* for the resigned version, publishing candid and posed photographs of each. Pain, considered to be one of the triggers of anguish, has a separate distinctive set of facial expressions[14,88] (page 20).

v Training in emotional skills[68] and compassion training[79] increases accuracy in recognizing facial expressions. An online interactive tool, the Micro Expression Training Tool (METT), which I developed, also increases accuracy in recognizing facial expressions in both normal and schizophrenic individuals (see www.paulekman.

com for METT and Russell[92] for the findings on schizophrenia) (page 20).

vi De Drue, 2012[25] (page 24).

vii Moll et al., 2006[82] (page 24).

viii I thank Clifford Saron for raising this question (page 24).

ix Preston & DeWaal's[87] "response *with* the object"; see also Miller, Caul, & Mirsky (1967);[81] and emotional contagion literature[58,59] (page 26).

x Dimberg, Andréasson, & Thunberg[30] recently found that the intensity of facial expression in response to seeing an emotional expression was related to the viewer's empathy (page 27).

xi Preston & de Waal[87] called this a "response *to* the object"; see also discussion of empathetic concern by Eisenberg & Fabes;[33] Carlo, Eisenberg, Troyer, Switzer, & Speer;[12] Eisenberg et al.[35] (page 30).

xii Clifford Saron raised this possibility (page 32).

xiii See Ekman & Davidson[44] for the major agreements and disagreements among those who study emotion (page 35).

xiv One emotion theorist, Nico Frijda, would disagree, as he posits that each emotion has as its central feature a different action tendency (page 36).

xv In a forced-choice paradigm, the most frequent response to posed facial expression of what was supposed to signal compassion was indeed compassion, but it was only 37%, with the other next most frequent responses: love, gratitude, and contentment. Free response rather than forced choice would be the preferred methodology, but has not been employed to date. Simon-Thomas, Keltner, Sauter, Sinicropi-Yao, & Abramson[96] report a vocal signal unique to compassion, but there is similar ambiguity about that evidence (page 37).

xvi While there have been attempts to establish a signal for shame and/or guilt, these require more than facial expression, or a sequence of movements, rather than the single configuration found for the seven emotions that have a universal facial expression[67] (page 37).

xvii Knafo, Zahn-Waxler, Van Hulle, Robinson, & Rhee (2008);[71] Warneken & Tomasello (2006);[102] Brownell (2013).[11] See Bloom[9] for a thoughtful discussion of this work and his own studies (page 42).

xviii For a very different discussion of heroism, see Franco & Zimbardo (2007);[48] Blau, Franco, & Zimbardo (2009);[8] and Franco, Blau, & Zimbardo (2011)[47] (page 43).

xix Whitehouse, Orne, & Dinges, 2002[104] (page 49).

xx LeDoux, 1998[72] (page 51).

xxi Ekman, 2003,[41] pp. 38–51 (page 51).

xxii See Ekman & Halpern (in review)[36] for a fuller discussion of these issues (page 69).

TOPIC INDEX

AUTHOR INDEX

CPSIA information can be obtained at www.ICGtesting.com
Printed in the USA
LVOW11s2236200616
493416LV00005B/147/P

9 780991 563609